Birding for Beginners Copyright © 2014 by Charles M. James

Birding for Beginners

By

Charles M. James

CONTENTS

4	Forward	
6	Chapter 1	Getting Started
11	Chapter 2	Crawl, Walk, Run
16	Chapter 3	My New Best Friend
22	Chapter 4	Eagle Eye
32	Chapter 5	Raptors
37	Chapter 6	Bird Feeders
43	Chapter 7	Pranksters
47	Chapter 8	The Usual Suspects
52	Chapter 9	New Areas
58	Chapter 10	What Else Is Out There
66	Chapter 11	They Quack Me Up
70	Chapter 12	Friends and Strangers
75	Chapter 13	Warblers
79	Chapter 14	Equipment
81	Chapter 15	Final Chapter
82	TIPS	
85	Index	

Forward

This is a labor of love for me. In my life I have had countless epiphanies that helped me grow and take my life experience to another level. In 2007 I was diagnosed with an aggressive form of prostate cancer. My doctors put together a very aggressive treatment plan that included radiation, isotope and chemo therapies. Although my current prognosis is good, I am still receiving treatments every three months. The treatments have caused physical changes in my life but more importantly psychological changes in my life.

My doctors warned me that I would have to exercise and watch my diet due to the weight gain side effects of my treatments. I didn't feel this would be an issue because a healthy lifestyle had always been an important part of my life. Weightlifting, jogging, and cycling were staples of my activities since childhood. I also have a love affair with Golf that borders on addiction. Besides, how many people get cancer and gain weight? LOL.

The reality was that my body underwent an extreme ordeal and my weight skyrocketed as my energy level dropped to an all-time low. I was not able to do the activities I was good at before the cancer. I tried to keep a positive attitude but I was now able to empathize with people on issues that I had never experienced up to that point. It was humbling to say the least but also good for my life journey. It is hard to walk in another man's shoes until you have to live it.

The shoes I have to walk in now forced me to make changes. I began to walk every day for at least an hour. This was hard coming from a time when I rode my bike 20-30 miles/day. During these walks I began to notice not only the sights around me but also the sounds. I would leave my front door and walk 1 ½ miles out and 1 ½ miles back. I would go in different directions every day to keep it interesting. It was a lot more fun than I imagined and I was treated to miracles every day. You don't have to make special trips to faraway places to get started birding.

I became very aware of the beautiful orchestra of sounds I heard during my walks. These sounds had to be there all of the time but were covered by my music, IPOD, and phone before the walks. I was very curious to find out where these sounds were coming from. Then it hit me. There were birds all around me. How could there have been so much activity so close to me and I was totally unaware of its existence? There were Robin Red Breasts and Sparrows singing joyfully as I walked. I began to take my camera on these walks and capture these birds. I have been taking pictures since I was about 10 years old. None of my knowledge would prepare me for the challenges of Bird Photography. I hope this book will help you in your Birding Journey. I tried to give the Tips I wish someone had told me to make this activity easier.

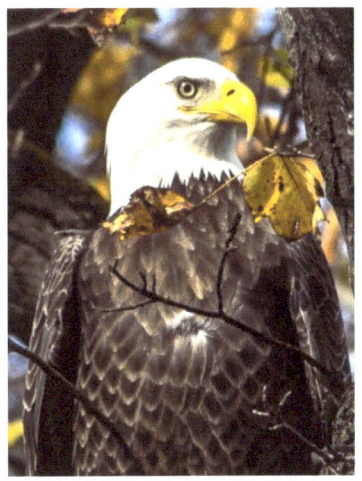

Chapter 1

Getting Started

Just do it. It is has become a cliché in our society but is good advice. Birding is very organic for me. Part of the fun is that I didn't approach it in the highly structured systematic way I usually use. It seemed to happen on its own without too much assistance from my conscious mind. Part of the fun is that I didn't have any expectations. I didn't go into it with the answer in mind. I felt like a child because I was able to discover something new and it was wondrous to me. I wanted to share what I saw and was excited every time I saw a new species of bird. I wanted to know what bird I had just seen when I didn't know what it was. **TIP#1-Keep it fun.** Birding doesn't have to be a job

I have gone on to read a lot about birding. I was well into my experience before I read any books on how to do it. To this day I don't own binoculars. They are a vital tool and I am not against them. I would suggest that you get the best equipment that you can afford. I started by just using my eyes. I think this is an advantage for me. There are a lot of species that are very small to the naked eye. Since I could not bring the birds in close with binoculars I had to learn to be stealth. It forced me to walk lightly and try to get close.

I also learned what to look for. It is a lot like buying a new car. After you buy one you notice how many cars like yours there are on the road. After I saw a species of bird for the first time I was more aware of that species. As I walked I would see a lot of a specific species I was familiar with. Without thinking about it, I was becoming more aware of where birds are in the trees and what type of trees I would see certain birds. I would notice if they were solitary or usually seen in groups. I found that different birds have different behaviors. I wanted to know what each species was like. It made it fun to see the same birds repeatedly in different lights. **TIP#2-You can learn a lot by just doing it.** This is how we learned as children and you will continue to improve your bird watching as time goes on. Each lesson will make the next lesson easier.

This is where my camera came into play. As a photographer I consider it my job to manipulate light and catch my subjects in interesting situations. All of my bird pictures were interesting since I didn't know much about them. I had to fight the urge to get a perfect picture and try to get any kind of picture. Birds usually don't pose. They move a lot and are quick in their movements. This makes it hard to get a perfect picture. I try to capture birds in interesting situations with perfect lighting but some of the pictures that have helped me identify birds are blurry and out of focus. **TIP#3-Birding doesn't lend itself well to perfection.** Look for the good in the pictures you take. The Northern Flicker below is a shot I saw out of the corner of my eye. I just wheeled around and took it instinctively. It is not the clearest photo but shows the beautiful gold shafts in its feathers.

Northern Flicker (Golden Shafted)

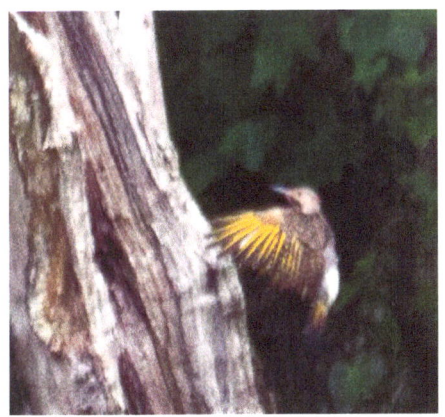 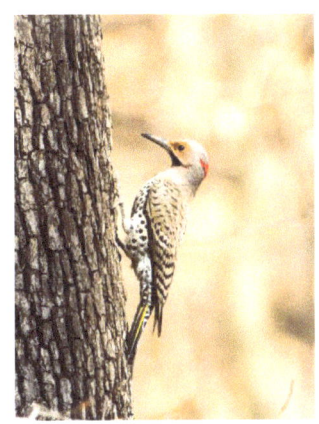

I began to walk everywhere and take my camera. I started to become very sensitive to motion and movement. I was walking back from the store one day and saw a big bird fly by out of the corner of my eye. It didn't look like anything I had ever seen before. As I looked in the large Sycamore tree to try and pick up the image of the bird it started to come into focus. It was amazing. I was looking at Woody Woodpecker. This huge black and white bird had a red crest on the top of his head. He was perched on a branch right in front of me. I was very excited. I had my camera and the lighting was right. **TIP #4-The lighting is best when you shoot down your shadow line.** To get the best light on the bird for a clear focused shot keep the sun at your back and shining directly on the subject. When you do this you will have the camera aimed down the line made by your shadow on the ground. A few degrees here or there aren't that important.

Pileated Woodpecker (male)

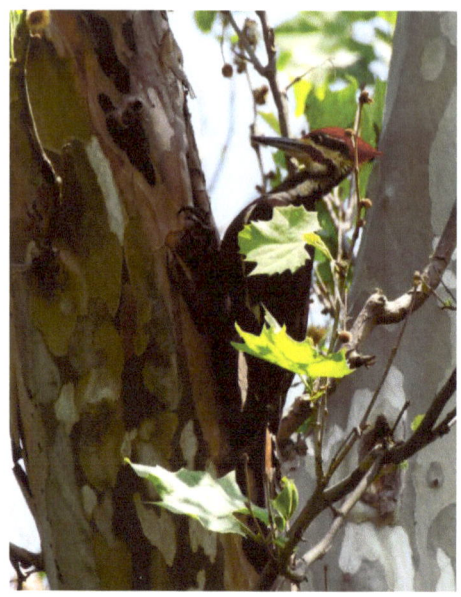

I got different shots as the woodpecker moved around the tree and interacted with the branches and lighting. I was able to zoom in close and continued to shoot. I wasn't sure how shutter speed and focal length would affect my pictures so I changed the settings on the camera to make sure I got good images. **TIP#5-Make sure you get a good shot before you start making changes to your camera settings.** If you aren't an advanced photographer use different settings when the birds are posing. Over time you will find out which settings give the best results in certain situations. I was so excited I rushed home and put the pictures into the computer.

The next day I went back to the same tree. After about 3 or 4 minutes I saw the same woodpecker again. I began to take a series of pictures. I was so focused on what I was shooting that I didn't notice that there was another woodpecker in the same tree. Now I reframed the shot and was taking two birds in the same frame. This was the first time this had happened to me and I was both surprised and pleased. I had never seen a real woodpecker in my life and now I was taking pictures of two at one time. How lucky was I to have had such a good experience. What had I done to deserve such a treat? I felt like I had received a gift and was thankful. Little Miracles Happen Every Day.

I wanted to include the shots I had of these woodpeckers in this book. Unfortunately I lost the pictures when my hard drive crashed. **TIP#6-Always back up your photos.** Hard drives are notorious for crashing so back up often. I learned this lesson the hard way.

When I got home and put the photos into the computer I realized that I had actually captured three woodpeckers in one of the shots. I went on the internet and discovered I had photographed a Pileated Woodpecker. I had captured a male, a female, and a juvenile. **TIP#7-Be aware of your surroundings.** Sometimes your field of view will reveal other birds that you won't see if you are too focused on one thing. I will contradict this tip later but it will make sense. LOL

The Pileated Woodpecker made me feel like a true birder. I had gotten a good photo session with a bird I thought was rare in my area. Later I would get many opportunities to photograph Pileated Woodpeckers. They are not rare here at all. I have never been as close or had the lighting as good as that first encounter. This is why I like birding. It is a new experience every time and you never know when you will get a once in a lifetime moment.

Chapter 2

Crawl, Walk, Run

You have to crawl before you walk. You have to walk before you run. We've all heard this before. This has not been my experience in Birding. I feel like I am crawling, walking and running at the same time. That is one of the things I like the most. There is still a lot I have to learn but there is a lot that I have already learned.

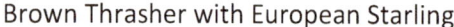

Brown Thrasher with European Starling

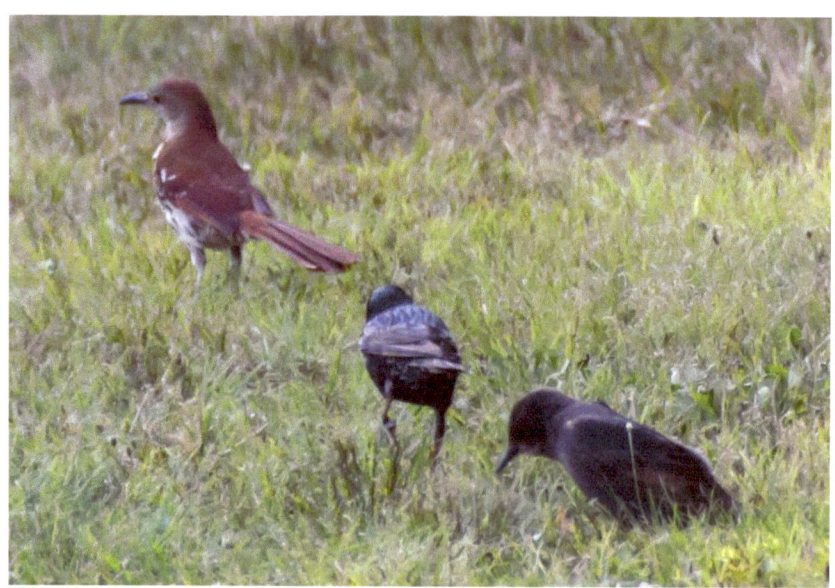

I used to look up for my best shots. Now I know that there are birds on the ground also. This might sound obvious but some of my favorite photos are of birds on the ground feeding. My best shot of a Brown Thrasher was taken while I was shooting European Starlings feeding on worms in a grassy field. As usual I was looking at one thing when something else came into focus. I didn't know what it was but knew I hadn't seen one before. I had to look it up when I got home and that is a fun part of the process. Learning what you don't know and adding the new information to your repertoire. After I saw my first Brown Thrasher I have seen many of them. Most of the time, they were on the ground or in thicket when I saw them. I didn't know how much time certain birds spend on the ground. Now I look on the ground and in the air. The tree canopy is the place to look for certain birds. The point is that there is no right place to look. Birding reminds me a lot of the art that used to be popular in my twenties. On the surface the picture looked like a pattern of nondescript colors. There is something hidden in the picture. When I looked for it I could never see anything different. When I relaxed my gaze the hidden image would just pop out at me.

One day I was looking for woodpeckers in an area where I had seen them many times before. I was looking at specific trees and areas where I thought they would be. All of the sudden a Red-shouldered Hawk appeared on a telephone line right in front of me. Not only was this a hawk I had never seen up close, he was posing. He looked right at me and didn't fly off. I got some really good pictures. I also noticed that this was a bird I had mistakenly identified as a Red Tailed Hawk .**TIP #8-Sometimes you have to relax your focus and let the Birds come to you.** You will have to focus on specifics and relax your focus at the same time. Birds are really camouflaged in their habitat and you have to learn to see them by relaxing. Since this experience I have seen many perched Hawks in places I would not have seen them last year.

Red-shouldered Hawk

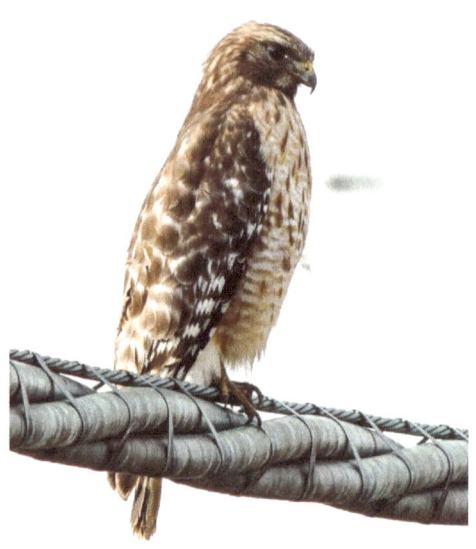

I have noticed that my birding skills have improved quickly. Some days it's as if I have never done it before. I miss shots that I had plenty of time to focus and get the correct lighting. Then other times I will catch something out of the corner of my eye and spin and get a great picture. **TIP#9-Don't beat yourself up if you miss a good picture.** Birding is a work in progress and each day will help you in the future. If you stay at it you will get another chance.

This process has made me feel as if I am crawling, walking, and running at the same time. I have learned the common names of many species of birds. I have not learned the formal names. At this point I am crawling here and am alright with this condition. My focus in birding is not based on the knowledge of the technical names and categories. I find it very impressive when people are able to speak in these terms but I have no interest in learning this right now. **TIP#10-Make your own decisions about your birding journey.** As you move forward you might change your mind about what is important to you. Do what you feel and what is most enjoyable at this moment.

I like to take pictures of large birds. We have a lot of hawks in my area. I think they are beautiful. They all have different styles of flight and look majestic as they survey the area from high above the ground. In my search for Hawks I have taken pictures of a lot of Vultures. Some people call them Buzzards. They are huge birds and don't have the same aura as hawks, falcons and eagles. As time has gone on I have come to appreciate Vultures. I now like the way they can soar effortlessly for hours in search of food. I was taking pictures of hawks one day when I came upon a flock Black Vultures perched in trees. I got some good photos. They have some very strange rituals when they are on the ground. It was very interesting. I have a new found interest in vultures. They also have helped me to identify other large birds in flight by noticing the differences in wing angle and flapping differences. **TIP#11-All birds can help you in your birding journey.** Looking for the similarities and differences in birds will make you a better birder.

Black Vultures

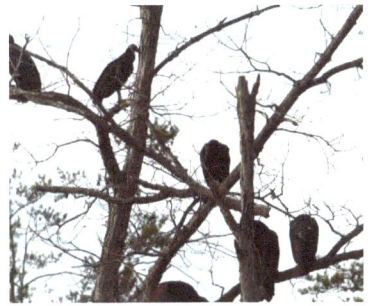

Black Vultures

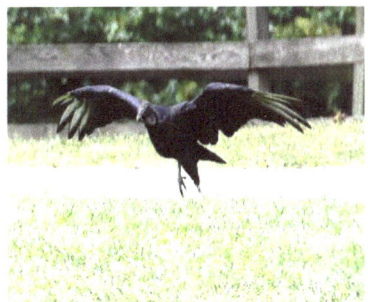

I wanted to get a picture of an American Bald Eagle. They are not very plentiful in the area where I live. I don't have any large bodies of water within the three miles from my house. I was starting to think about trips where I could go to increase my chances of getting a good photograph. I started to ask people in the area if they had ever seen an American Bald Eagle. I was told of the occasional sighting in our area but not too many places where they were seen frequently. I started to walk to all of the areas where anyone told me they had seen Eagles. I was disappointed that I was not having any luck seeing this regal symbol of our country. One day I was editing some photos of Black Vultures I had taken near my house. I zoomed in and was separating the birds out into individual pictures. To my surprise I had captured an American Bald Eagle and didn't even know it. I had already accomplished something I wanted and wasn't aware of it. The lowly vulture had helped me to get what I wanted without my knowledge. **TIP#12-When you take group bird pictures, make sure you check every individual bird.** After this experience I went back and checked many of my shot to find birds I had not identified before. I call these freebees. Some birds travel in small numbers with flocks of other birds.

American Bald Eagle

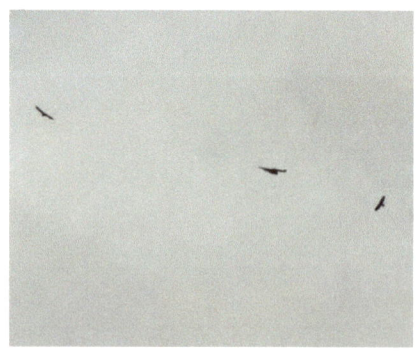
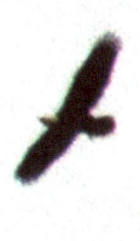

Chapter 3

My New Best Friend

Great Blue Heron

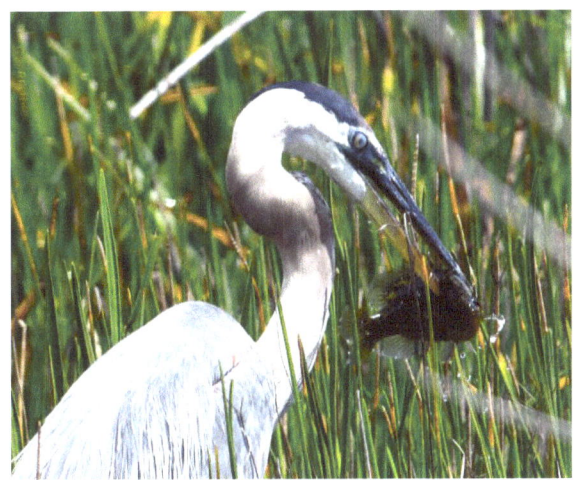

During my walks I got better at seeing birds that were hidden to me earlier. I spent a lot of time at small ponds. These ponds are all along the bike path near my house. I have gotten good shots of Great Blue Herons. I have come to love this huge bird. By frequenting the ponds I learned how to set up the camera to get good still and action shots of this huge bird. One day I was looking for Herons and heard a really strange noise. The source of the sound was a medium sized bird I had never seen before. This was a beautiful bird with blue, white and reddish colors. I was captivated by this bird and spent about an hour watching and taking photos of it. After a while I saw another one in the same area. When I got home I found that my new friend was a Belted Kingfisher. I was so fixed on the male that I didn't notice the other one on the tree.

Over the next few weeks I had a number of encounters with these magnificent birds. The kingfisher has become my new best friend. I got some very good pictures and even some good video. **TIP#13-Many different species of birds frequent the same habitat.** Ponds are especially good places to check out and spend time carefully examining the area.

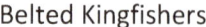

Belted Kingfishers

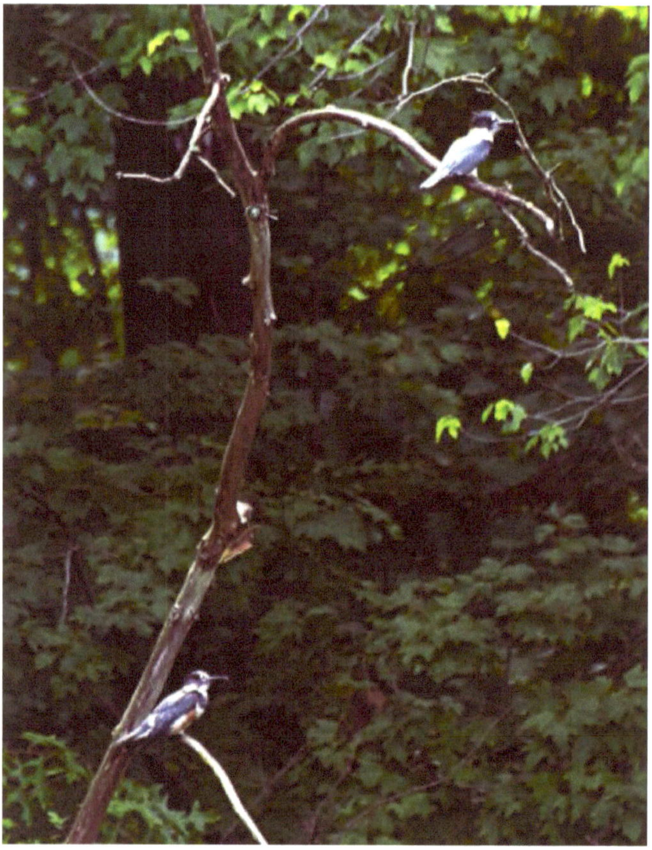

Belted Kingfisher (female)

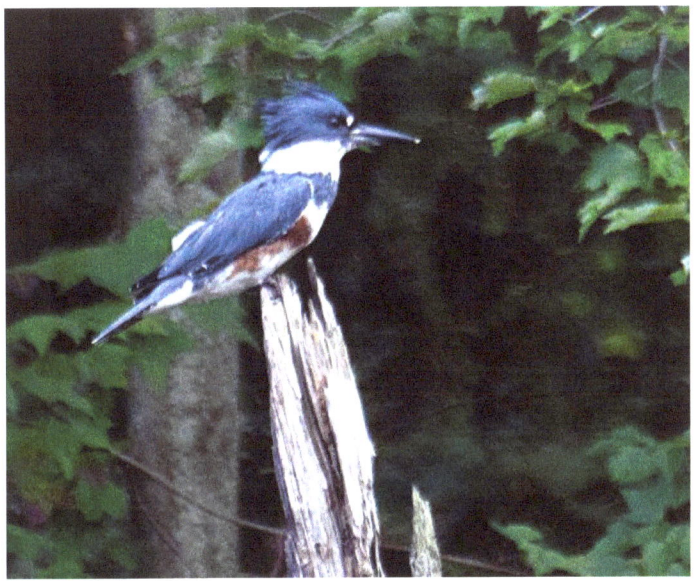

I learned that Belted Kingfishers love crawfish. They will beat the crawfish on a tree branch to kill it before they eat it. From time to time it will toss the crawfish in the air and catch it to change his grip. What a showman.

    One day I was taking pictures of the Belted Kingfisher when I saw a very strange looking bird. It had a head like a Heron but was very different from a Great Blue Heron. The lighting was good and I got a lot of good shots. When I got home I looked it up and found out my new surprise was a Green Heron. The Green Heron will stand very still when they hunt for fish. This is a good bird to shoot using a tripod. **TIP#14 –Use a tripod if you can to get the best pictures.** If you have a remote shutter release it is even better. Even cameras with Image Stabilization will sometimes have slight lens blur from camera motion even though the stabilization appears to stops the action. I will admit that a tripod cramps my style but you can't beat the results. Now that I have some very good pictures of many birds I am trying to get great pictures. The tripod has helped when the birds cooperate.

Green Heron (male)

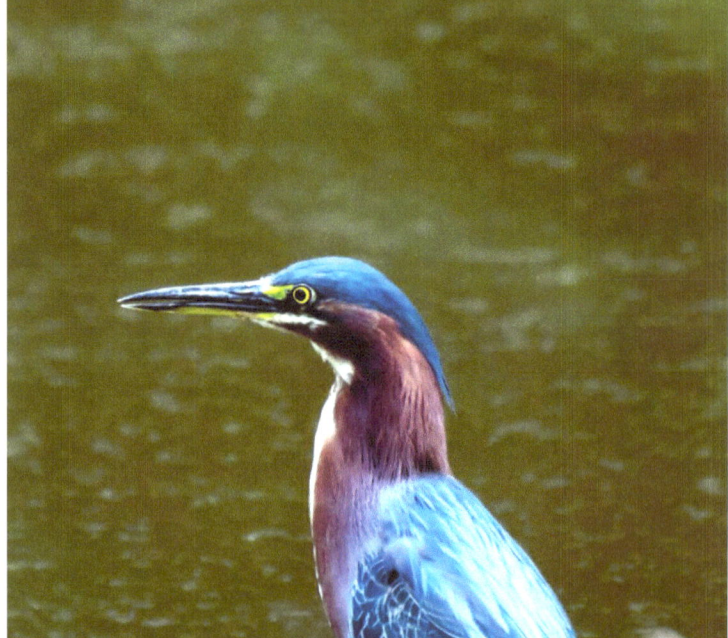

Green Herons have a crest on their head that does a weird thing when they are excited. This is one of the things I learned by watching and trying to get interesting photos.

Green Heron (male)

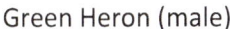

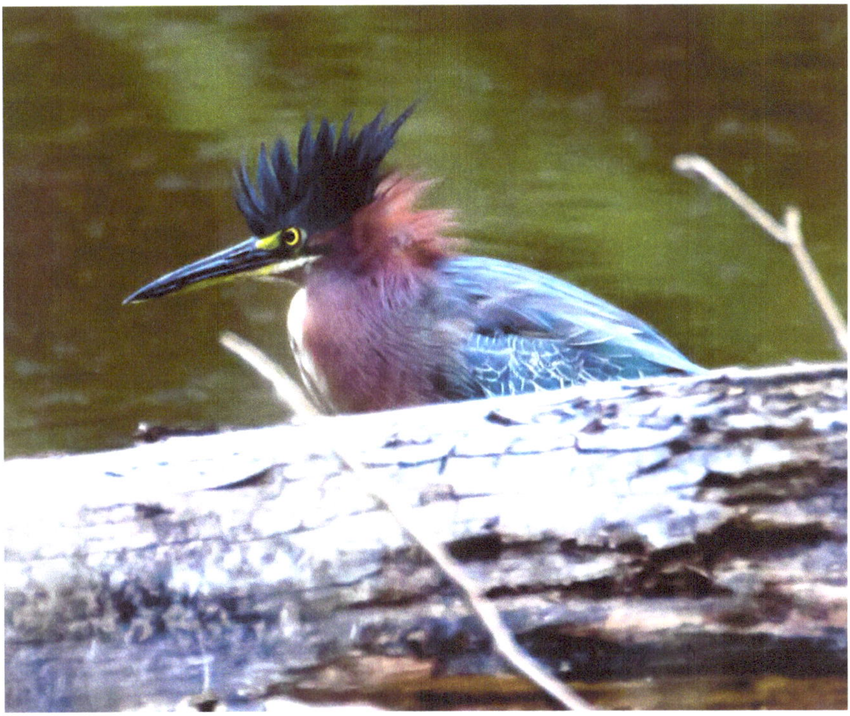

Like many other bird species the male is the most colorful. I have gotten good pictures of the Green Heron now that I know what to look for.

I thought I would get a lot of pictures of ducks but it didn't work out that way. For this reason I am always happy to get pictures of ducks.

I later learned that many ducks migrate into our area and are only here at certain times of year. I came upon this duck at the same pond where I got my kingfishers and herons. It was hard to identify what type of duck it was. The difference between males and females can sometimes make identification difficult. When I got home I incorrectly identified the duck as an American Black Duck. Since that time I have read up and found that it was a female Mallard Duck. **TIP#15-There is a lot of information out there about birds.** I use a variety of sources from books to the internet to other birders. I plan to go to the Audubon Society to see if they can help me identify my unknown pictures.

Mallard Duck (female)

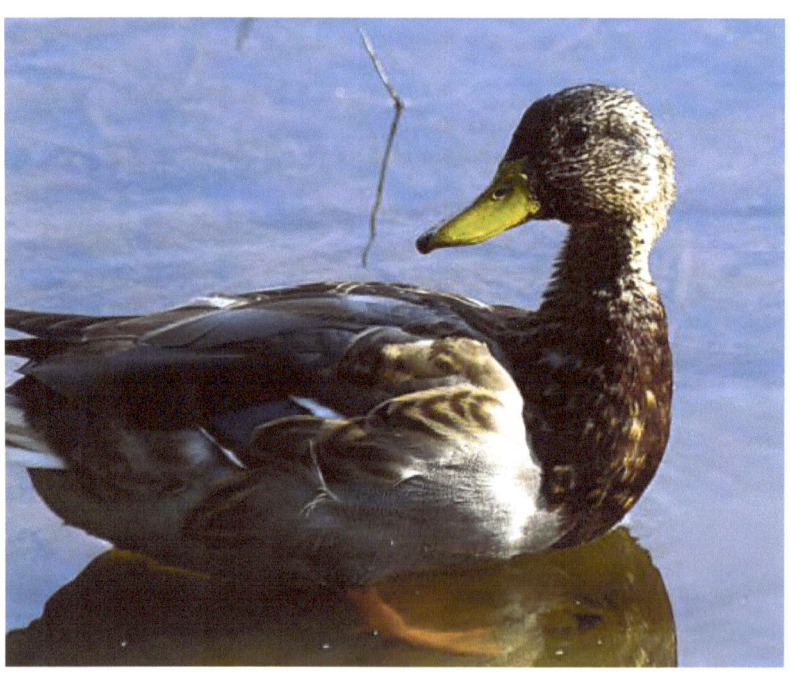

Chapter 4

Eagle Eye

It is hard to get a good sense of the size of birds from a distance. In the beginning of my birding I used to wonder how big a bird was that I saw off in the distance. This is one of the skills that have been hardest to develop. To get good at it you have to study the things that make birds different from each other. Color is important but so is size. Most field guides help you with field markings to identify birds. These clues aren't as obvious at a distance as it is up close. I started to pay attention to the songs and voices of birds. Lately I have paid more attention to the posture of certain birds. **TIP#16-Sometimes you have to put a lot of variables together to identify a bird at a distance.** This is one of my favorite parts of birding. I am trying to develop my Eagle Eye. I spot birds only by eye. This is about the equivalent of a 28mm lens on a full frame camera and about 18mm on a crop sensor camera. The next photos were shot with a 300mm lens. This is about a 14x magnification. Finally I will show what I saw on the computer after 100% crop. From the photos you can see why Bird Photography is so difficult. I am still pleasantly surprised when I get home and load my pictures into the computer. Sometimes the bird is eating something or interacting with something. This level of detail was lost to me when I took the picture. For this reason you should try to get as close to the bird as possible. It would seem that getting a bigger lens would be the answer. The problem is that it is hard to pick up the bird after the lens gets over about 500mm. These lenses are also very expensive and very heavy.

Blue Jay shot with 300mm lens

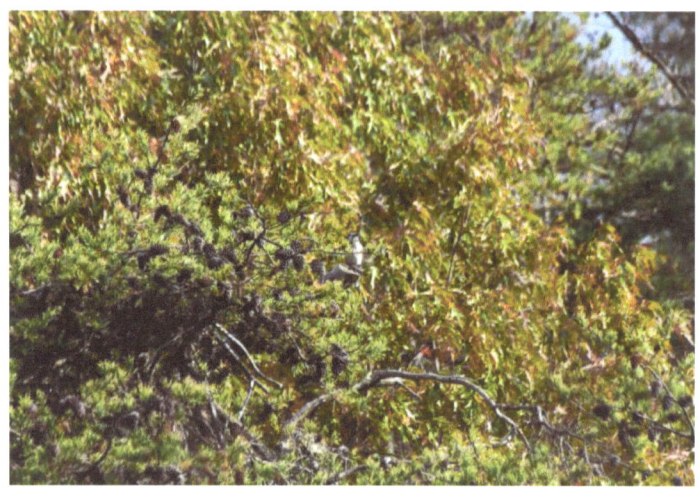

Same shot 100% Crop

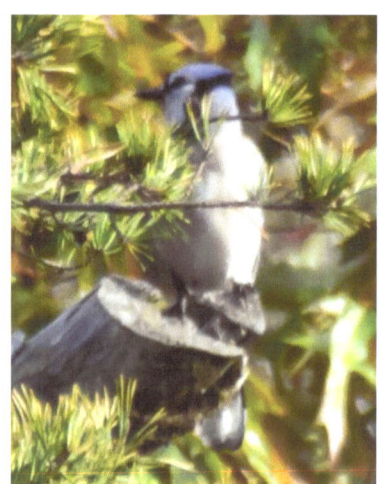

Blue Jay shot with 300mm lens

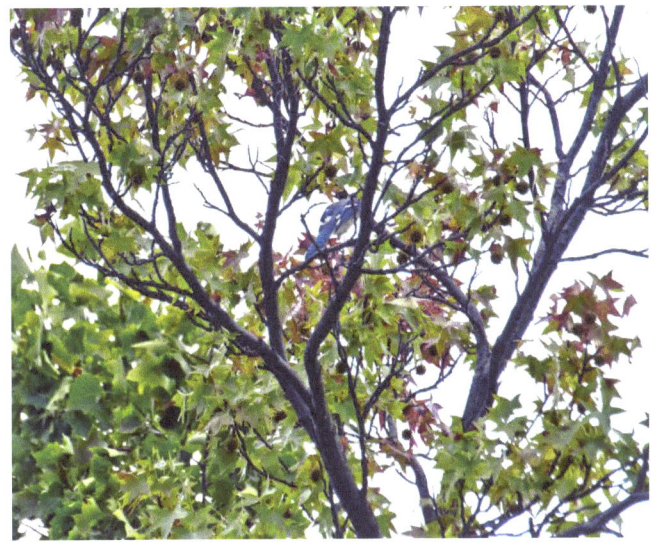

Same shot 100% Crop

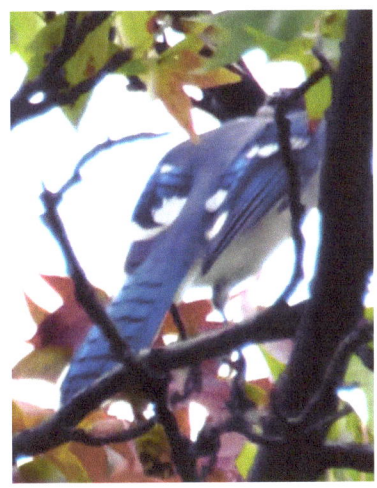

Blue Jay shot with 300mm lens

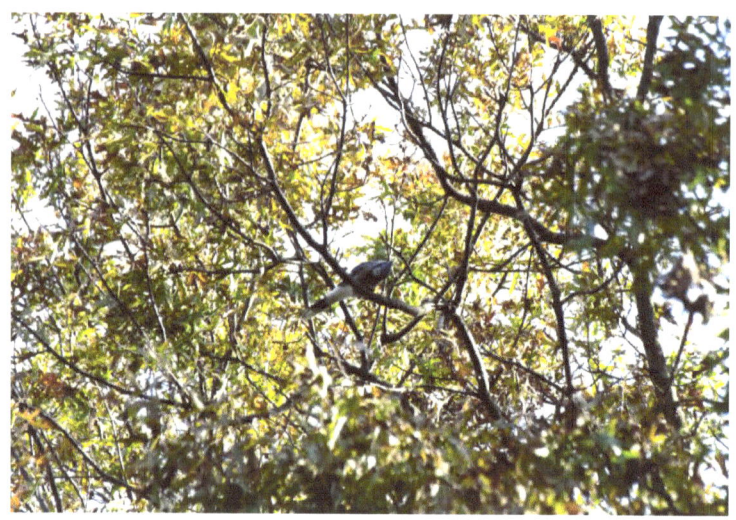

Same shot 100% Crop

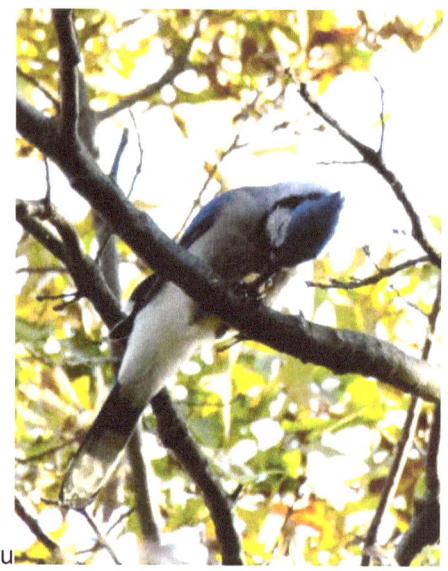

Bird feeders are a good way to observe birds up close and get clues that will help you at a distance. After putting up my hummingbird feeders I got better at seeing the hummingbirds when they were in flight. Then I learned that they perch in trees just like they do on the feeders. I was able to get some good natural pictures when I was able to follow their flight. There was a time when I didn't have any hummingbird pictures. Once I had an idea of their behavior it made seeing them easier.

Ruby-throated Hummingbird (female)

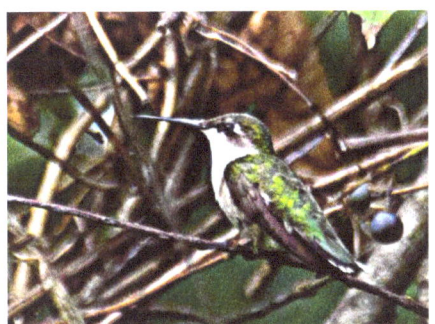 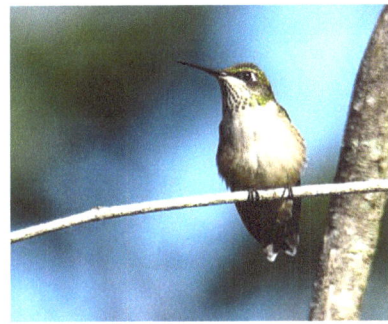

I credit a lot of my success with hummingbirds to butterflies. On some of my slow bird days I would photograph butterflies. After a while I could get their speed and patterns down pat. Being able to anticipate where they would land helped me get good pix.

TIP#17-Learn to anticipate where the bird will land for better photos. This is especially important for birds that don't usually pose.

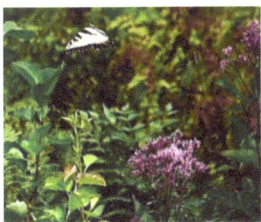 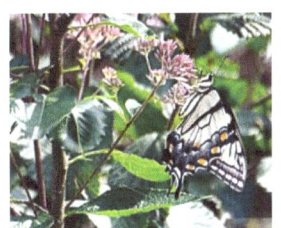

One bird that I found hard to get a good shot of is the Downey Woodpecker. The first time I saw this bird I was hot on the trail of a Blue Jay that frequented my back yard. I had seen this Blue Jay many times but he eluded me and my camera for weeks. On this day I had gotten a partial of him and at that time it was my best Blue Jay picture. As I improved my position to get a better shot I saw this small bird flitting from branch to branch. It was very small and quick. The colors were vibrant black and white with a touch of red on the back of the head. I tried to anticipate his moves but he was definitely hyperactive. I had a picture of the Pileated Woodpecker and the Northern Flicker but was unaware of the other Woodpeckers in my area. My expectation was keeping me from seeing them even though they we were all around.

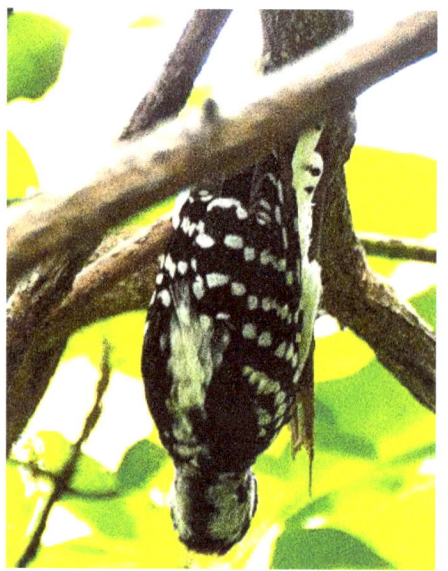

This bird followed the usual pattern. After I saw it the first time I continued to see it more and more. I learned how to spot it and what position it liked in the trees. It is one of the few birds that will hang upside down in the tree. This brings me to my next tip. **TIP#18- Sometimes you have to let the action come to you.** I was walking to one of my best spots when I saw a group of bushes and vines where there was a lot of bird activity. I stopped in this spot and set up a tripod. After about 10 minutes of standing very still I got this shot. A Downey Woodpecker came right to me and gave me an opportunity to get some good shots. I think he was after the same berries that some of the other birds were after. I have used this tactic many times with good results.

Downey Woodpecker (male)

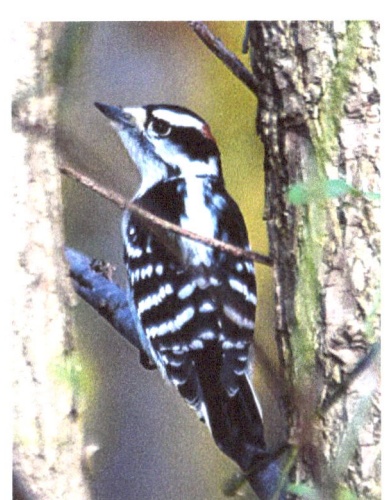 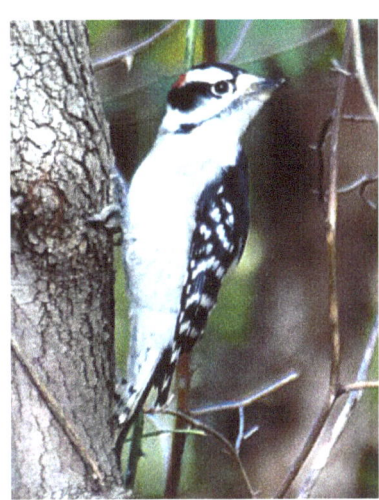

Now I had the Pileated and Downey Woodpeckers in my collection. I had only seen the Northern Flicker one time and didn't know it was in the woodpecker family. I went on a mission to find the Northern Flickers and get more pictures of them. It wouldn't take long before I found them. I was walking the path where I had seen a lot of hawks. I kept hearing the cooing sound similar to the sounds made by pigeons.

When I localized the sound it was coming from a Northern Flicker on a dead tree. It was far away from me but at this point I was happy just to get more pictures of this bird.

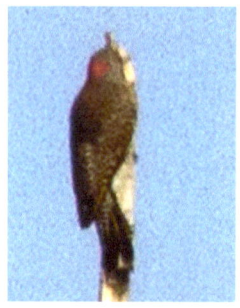 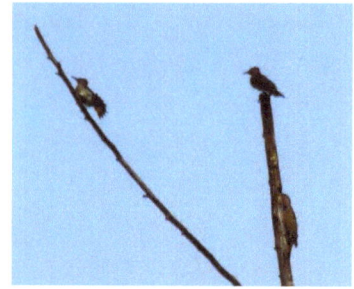

Then something very exciting happened. Another Northern Flicker flew to a nearby tree. I had only seen one of these birds and now I saw two. I couldn't believe it. Then a third one flew onto the tree. This is the trifecta of birding. Similar events like this have happened to me since I began birding. I always see it as a small miracle and a reminder of the beauty and splendor of the nature that is all around us. **TIP#19-Little Miracles happen every day.** This is one of the joys of birding and can keep you motivated to continue your journey. These moments reinforce the spiritual aspects of the journey I am now on.

Now I wanted more woodpeckers. When I was a child I heard people talk about Yellow-Bellied Sapsuckers. I had no idea it was a woodpecker. I wanted to get a picture because I heard we had them in my area. While I was looking for Pileated Woodpeckers in a park near my house I saw this bird. I didn't know what it was but that it had to be a woodpecker. When I got home I looked in my National Geographic book and saw it was a Yellow-Bellied Sapsucker. This is a beautiful bird because of the combination of colors. The red crown and the red throat stand out against the white and gold colors with black base.

Yellow-Bellied Sapsucker (male)   Yellow-Bellied Sapsucker (male)

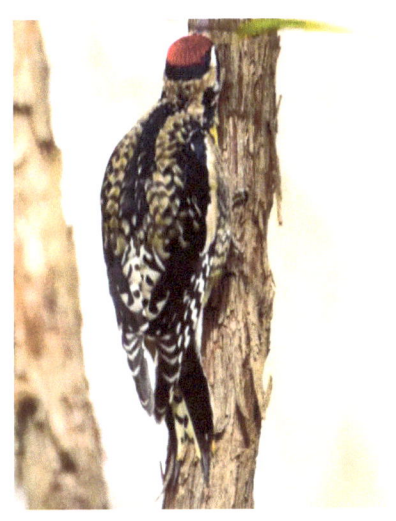
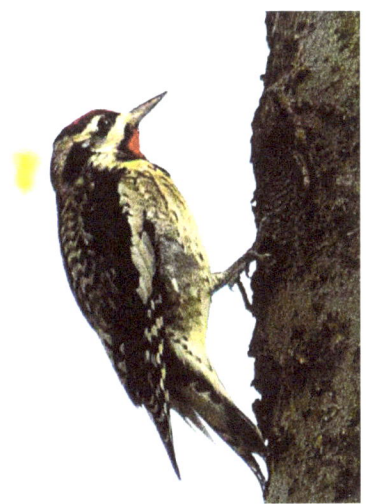

Now that I had this woodpecker I had to add two more to the list. The Red-Bellied Woodpecker and the Hairy Woodpecker. I read that the Hairy Woodpecker was similar to the Downey Woodpecker. One way to tell the difference is the length of the beek. Notice how the beek of the Downey on the right is about half the length of the head. The Hairy on the left has a beek that is the same length as the head. **TIP#20-Keep a folder of Birds you can't identify for further study.** I went back to my Downey Woodpecker pictures and found a picture of a Hairy Woodpecker mixed in. This was great. A new species right under my nose. I like the sections on similar species in the National Geographic book. My wife bought it for me so it is especially important to me. **TIP#21-Birding is an activity that you can involve your entire family.** I like every aspect of birding. My family doesn't like the long hikes but enjoy helping me identify the birds when I get back home after taking picures. My son likes to take pictures of the birds at the feeders. Maybe at some point he will go with me on the hikes.

Hairy Woodpecker   Downey Woodpecker

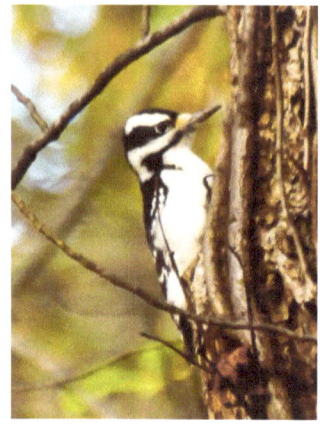
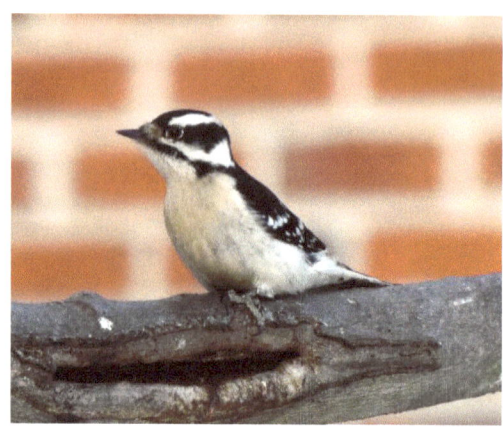

    One down, one to go. I looked in various books so that I would know when I got a chance for a Red-bellied Woodpecker. It didn't take long to get one. The area where I got the Yellow-Bellied Sapsucker was a woodpecker haven. I would always see a lot of them in this park. On the day when I got my Red-Bellied Woodpecker I had already photographed Pileated and Downey Woodpeckers. The Red Bellied Woodpecker has a red stripe on his head but doesn't have any distinct red on his belly.

Red-bellied Woodpecker

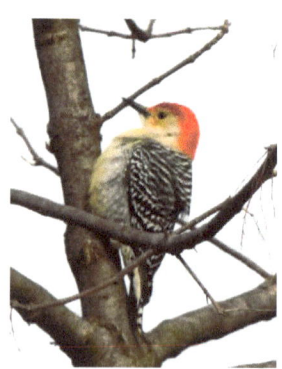

CHAPTER 5

Raptors

After my experience with the Woodpeckers I was feeling confident. I put it in my mind to find the Large Predators. I wanted to hunt down some hawks and eagles. I knew there were a lot of hawks around and I had already gotten an eagle by accident. I didn't have a clue of where to find them but I was hopeful they would find me. I was walking a path that I usually only walked for exercise. There were not many ponds on this section so I though there wouldn't be many Accipiter opportunities. On the way back home I heard what sounded like hawk noises from the woods on my left. I wasn't very hopeful because I had been fooled by mockingbirds and Blue Jays that mimmick hawks. I tried to localize the sound but the woods were thick. All of the sudden I saw a hawk fly towards me and into the woods. I tried to follow him and get pictures but they didn't turn out well. I was happy to have seen the hawk and felt I would be ready the next time I got a chance. **TIP#22-Set up your camera for two different shooting conditions. Full screen Focus and Single point Focus.** The first is good when you don't have a specific subject. I use it to get flying birds when they come up on me quickly. I call the second set up sniper mode. I used this mode for the picture on the right to get the bird in focus through the leaves that are out of focus. If you have time you will usually get a better picture in the sniper mode but you will not always have the time to get such a clear shot.

Red-tailed Hawk

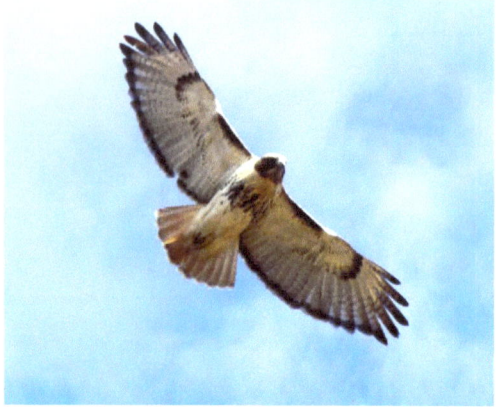
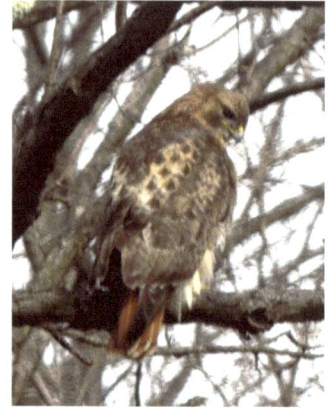

Also notice that the lighting is not the best in either picture. Sometimes you will not get a perfect picture. Remember **TIP#3.** If you stay at it you will get another opportunity. Here is a recent sequence I took of a Red-shouldered Hawk. He posed and I got very close to him and had the sun in the right place.

Red-shouldered Hawk

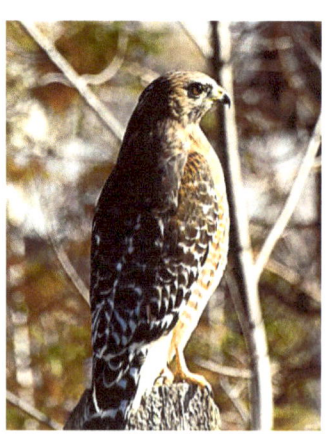
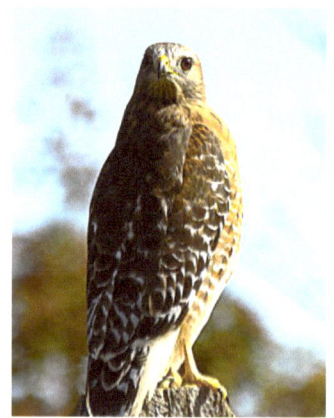

I had my hawk and now was ready to get some good pictures of an American Bald Eagle. I was told there was an occasional sighting of eagles at a water reserve near my house. I decided to check it out one Saturday. It was a beautiful place on the Anacostia River near Washington, DC. There were a lot of sea gulls there. I took some pictures of them. I also got some pictures of Double-crested Cormorants. This was a new species for me. I was having such a good day I lost track of the fact I was there to get an eagle picture.

After taking more gull pictures an American Bald Eagle flew overhead. I was so excited I couldn't get the camera focused at first. I lost all of my cool. I was hoping it would stay long enough for me to get one good shot. After I got the first one it was a lot easier. I finally had my eagle shots. **TIP#23-Enjoy the moment.**

American Bald Eagle

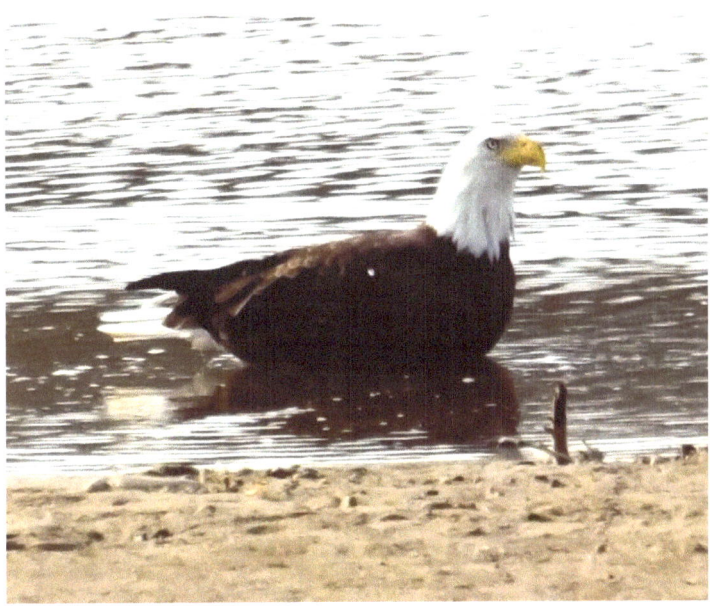

I would be remiss if I left the predators without talking about the Osprey. I used to fish for bass a lot. The Osprey used to fish the same spots. One day I called my wife and asked her to bring my camera to where I was fishing. She obliged and I got some good shots. I was not into Birding at the time but he was so beautiful and majestic that I had to get a picture.

I was happy with the shots but put them aside. I started to carry my camera with me when I went fishing. On this particular day everything went my way. I caught a lot of large bass. Then an Osprey showed up and posed for me until I got the series of pictures below. To this day this is one of my best series of pictures and this made the Osprey one of my favorites. **TIP# 24- Follow the Boy Scout Pledge and always be prepared. You never know when you will get the chance of a lifetime.**

Osprey

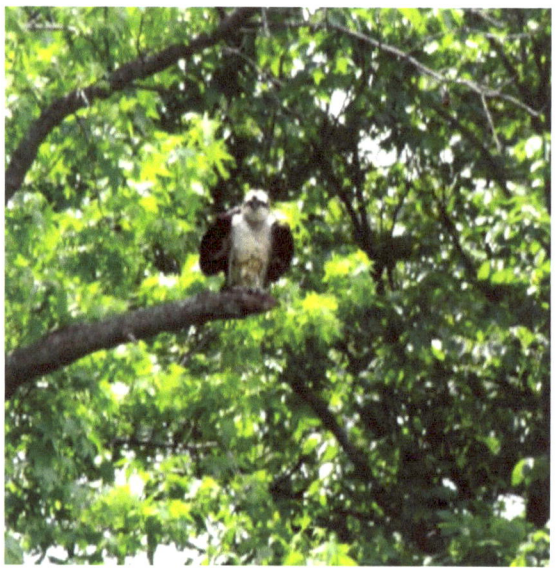

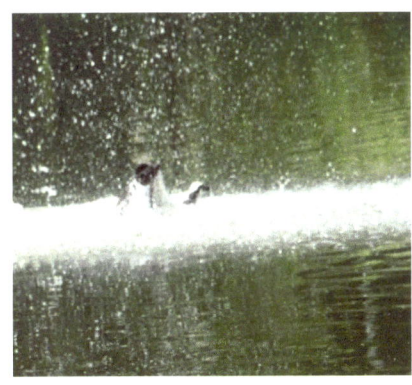
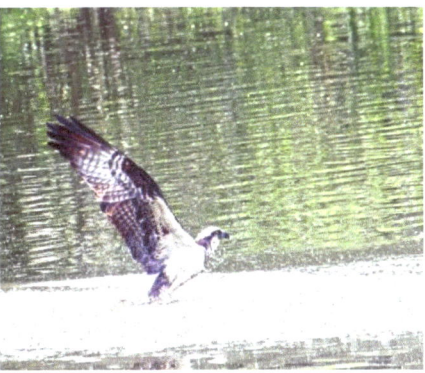

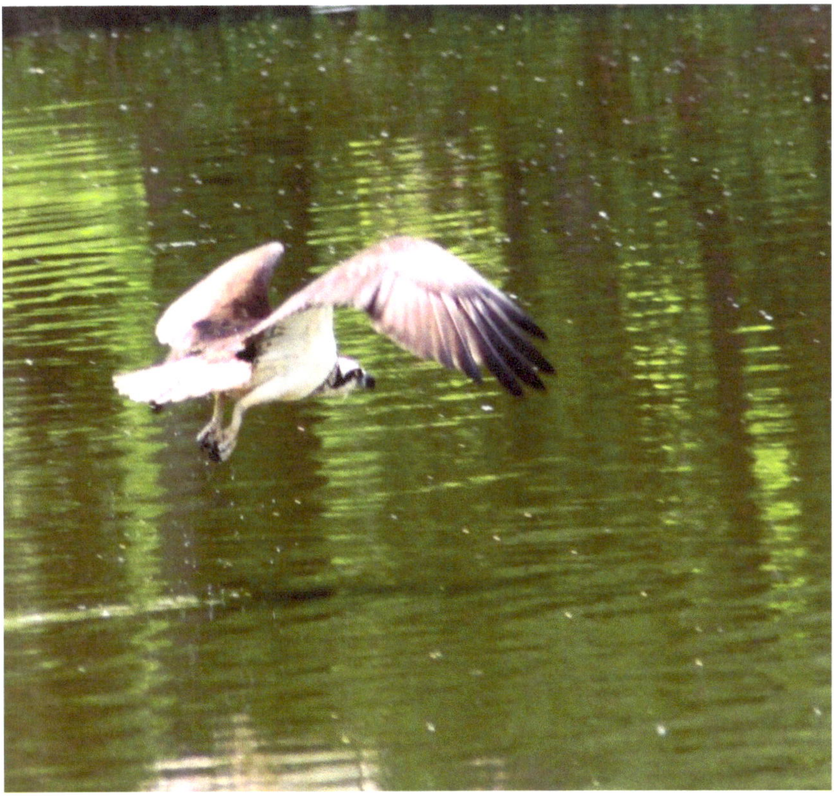

Chapter 6

Bird Feeders

On one of my regular walk routes there is a beautiful house on a large lot. There is a large bird feeder and bird bath in the yard that introduced me to a lot of new species. My first finch and titmouse were taken at this feeder. This became one of my favorite spots. **TIP#25-Its not cheating to get great pictures at a birdfeeder.** Up to this point I was in love with the big birds. Now I was becoming intrigued by some of the smaller birds.

The House Finches are very pretty birds. I haven't seen many in the wild. I have also seen Tufted Titmouse and Woodpeckers at this feeder. The Northern Cardinal was another regular. One of my favorites is the American Goldfinch. The males are very colorful and look like tropical birds.

American Goldfinch and House Finch

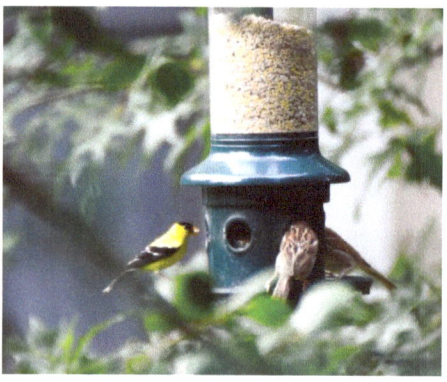

It is rare to see the birds play nice. Some of the birds are very territorial and chase any intruders away.

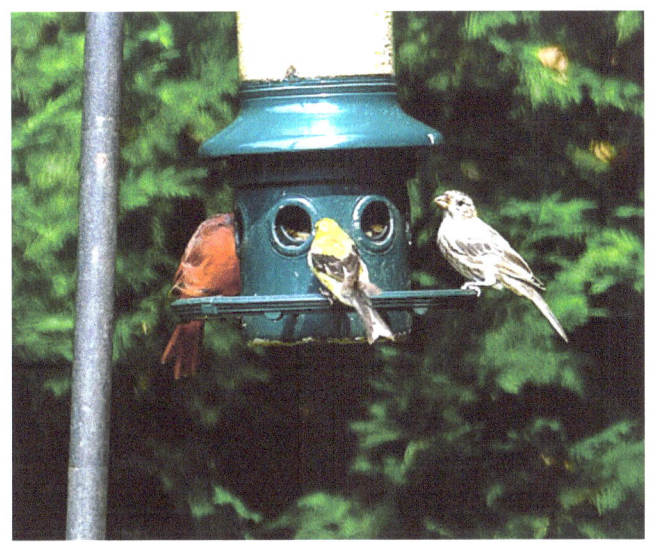

Purple Finch

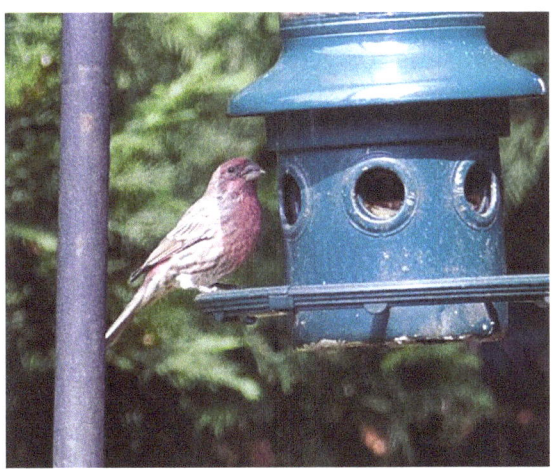

I now have my own feeders. This has brought birds to my house that weren't there before. The white-breasted nuthatch is a cool bird. He will hang upside down like the Downey Woodpecker. They are very active birds and don't pose very often. They will come for seeds and like the Suet Feeders.

White-Breasted Nuthatch

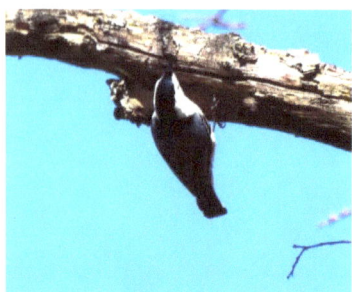
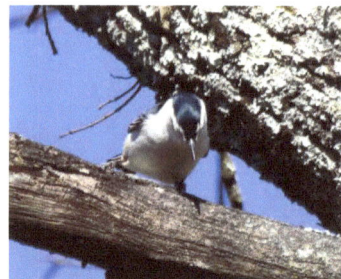

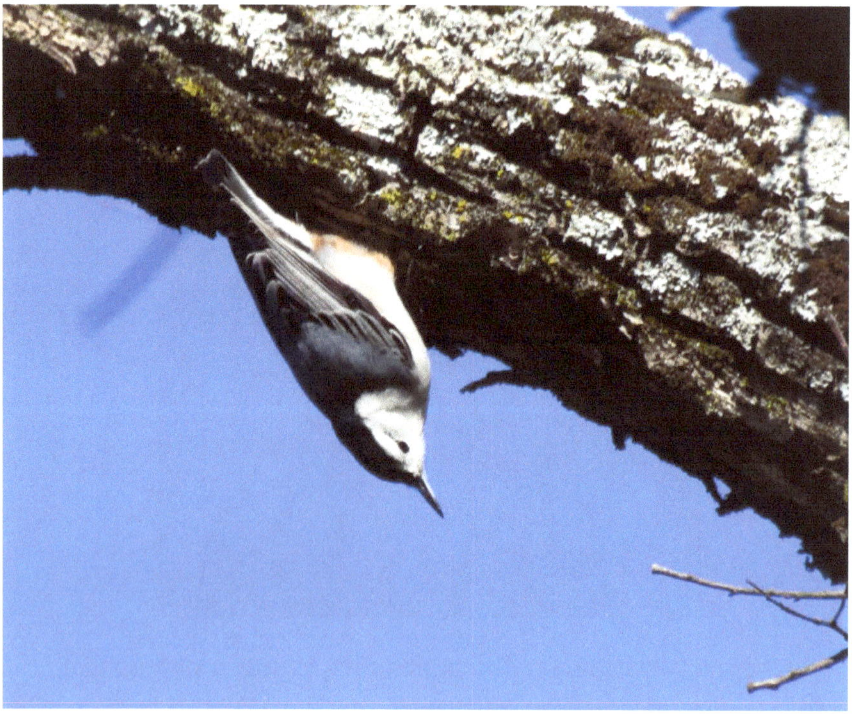

One day I saw this cute little bird chasing a Tufted Titmouse away from the feeder every time he attempted to eat. The Tufted Titmouse is a small bird. I have seen them after this but they

Tufted Titmouse

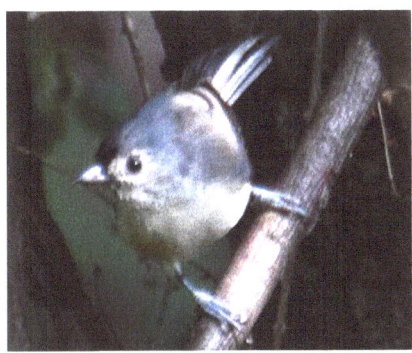 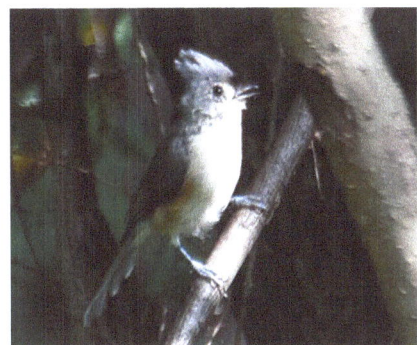

are usually more hidden in the cover. I was glad I had a good picture. This picture put me on a small bird mission. I love the large birds and trying to find them. Now I wanted to get good pictures of the smaller birds. This would prove to be a bigger challenge than I expected. I had gotten photos at the bird feeder and now wanted to catch them in a more natural setting.

One day I walked upon a bird I could not identify. It was about the size of a Tufted Titmouse but didn't have the tuft. It was hard to get a good picture. I had to stay still and wait for the bird to get into a position where I could get these shots. Later I identified this bird as a Ruby-crowned Kinglet. I found out there is a Golden-crown Kinglet also.

Ruby-crowned Kinglet

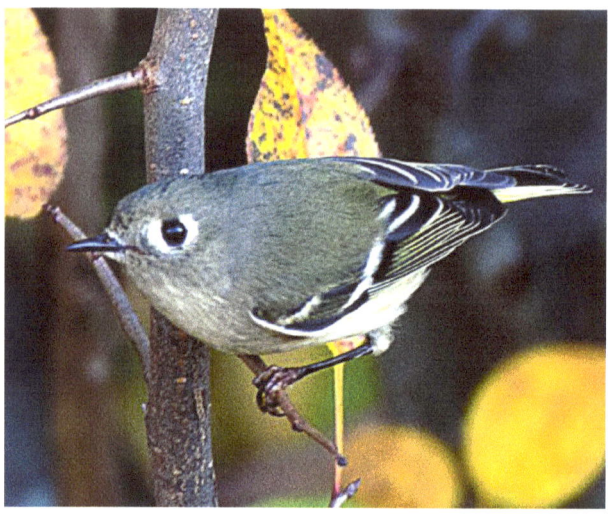

Now that I had captured a Ruby-crowned Kinglet I wanted to find a Golden-crowned Kinglet. It took a while but I saw a small flock of them on one of my walks. I think time of year was a key to getting this bird. I hadn't seen them during the spring and summer. This was a fall day and there was a lot of activity in this area.

Golden-Crowned Kinglet

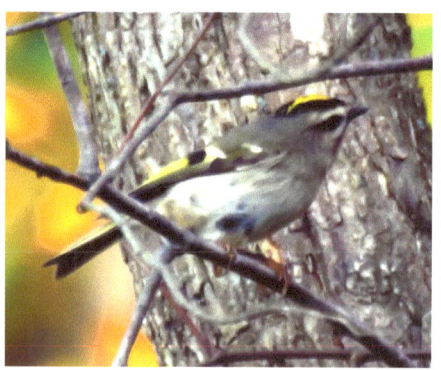

This bird has a very peculiar behavior. They will hover like a hummingbird to excite the insects. Then they will perch on the tree and eat them. It took me a while to figure out what they were doing. It was kind of cool. One of the pictures below captures this behavior. **TIP#26-Learning a birds behavior will help you to get more interesting pictures.** I knew if I was patient and used my camera's burst mode I would get the picture I wanted.

Golden-crowned Kinglet

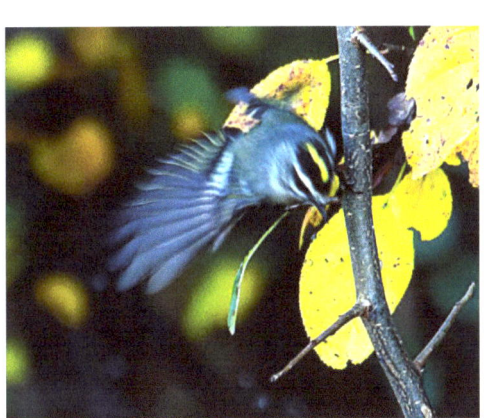

Many times you know the type of picture you want. If you want the bird clear and free of blur motion you need a fast shutter speed. I prefer 1/1600 or better. This will also give you less lens motion blur. If you want some motion blur that shows wing movement you might try around 1/500 or faster. Be aware that if you have to set your ISO setting above 1600 to get these high shutter speeds you will increase the noise in the picture. This will be more obvious the more you crop the picture.

Large birds create their challenges when trying to get a good photo. Small birds are also full of challenges. The good news is that you can get really close to the small birds when you learn patience.

Chapter 7

Pranksters

Some birds seem to have swag. They like to annoy the other birds. They are usually very vocal and like to be heard as well as seen.

Northern Mocking birds are very plentiful in my area. I have a lot of shots of them. Recently, I set up a tripod and waited at a spot where I have seen these birds in the past. Here is one of the pictures I got. I was very happy with the detail that was missing in some of my earlier shots.

Northern Mockingbird

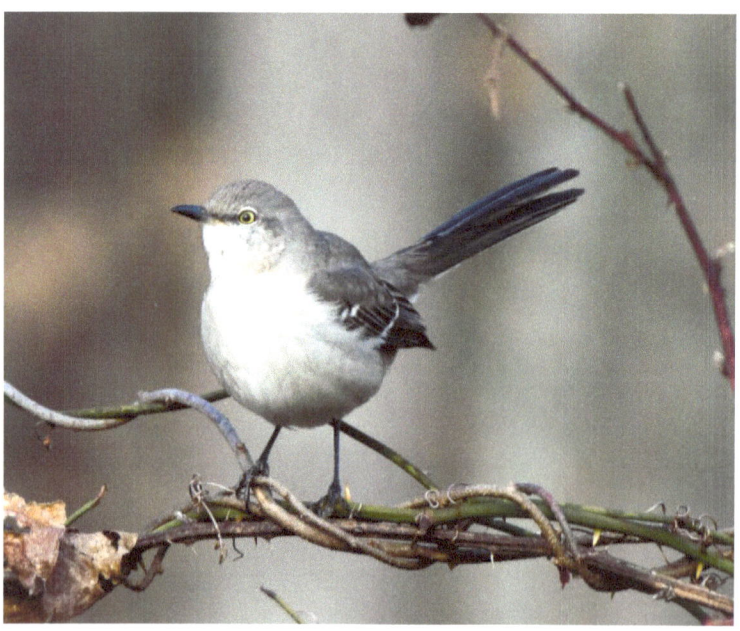

The Northern Mockingbird has fooled me on a number of ocassions. These birds mimick other birds. I have noticed that they mimick hawks when I get near their nests. They also mimick the song birds. I think I am going to get a good picture of a sparrow only to find out it is a Northern Mockingbird. They have a lot in common with the Gray Catbird. These birds also mimick other birds. They also mimick cats which is how they got their name.

Gray Catbird

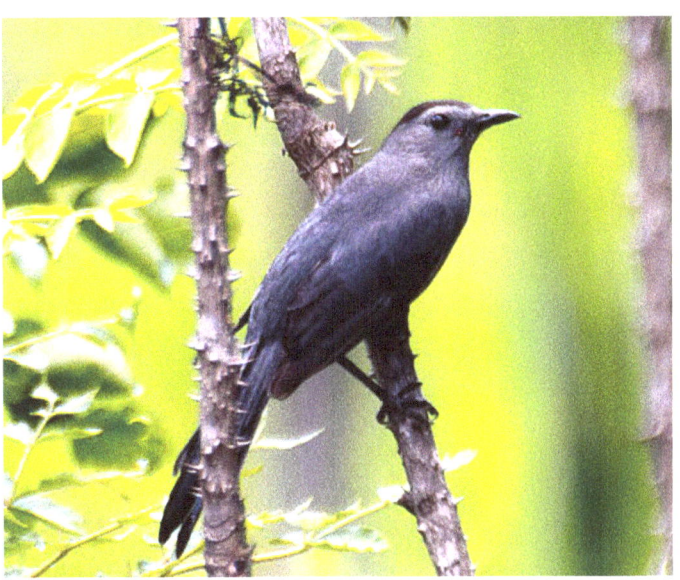

I would put crows in this segment. There are a lot of American Crows in my area. I really took them for granted. I would photograph them on occasion but felt like I could get them anytime. One day I was shooting a Red Shouldered Hawk and saw a crow dive bombing the Hawk. This made me more interested in the American Crow. Who is this bird that isn't afraid of a Hawk? They seem to be pranksters and like to mess with the other birds. I was shooting Gulls one day and the American

Crows were always bothering them. They would fly to where the gulls were perched and chase them to another place. This was funny to me because the gulls do this to each other a lot. The American Crow is a large bird but not compared to the Ring-billed Gull

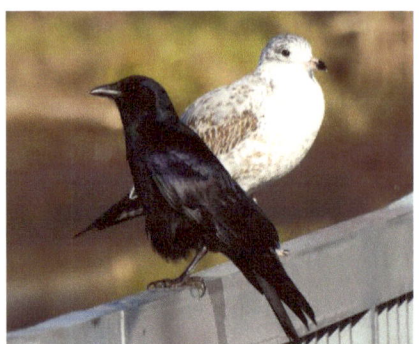 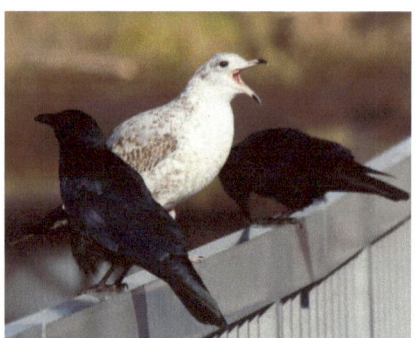

American Crow

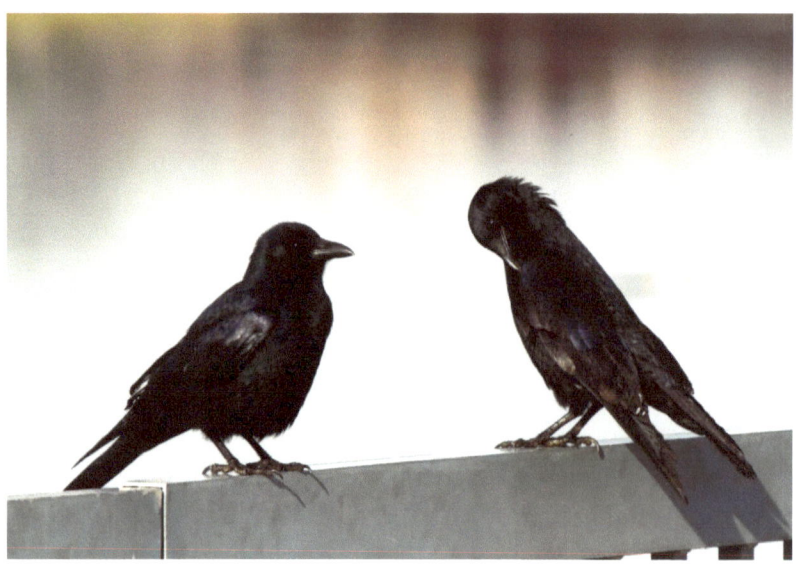

I like the gulls because they frequent a spot where I go to look for eagles. The gulls are always doing something. Sometimes they will get an object, fly off with it and drop it. After flying down to retrieve it they will start the process again. There is a large Greater Black-backed Gull that seems very dominant with the other gulls. Below he did what dominants do.

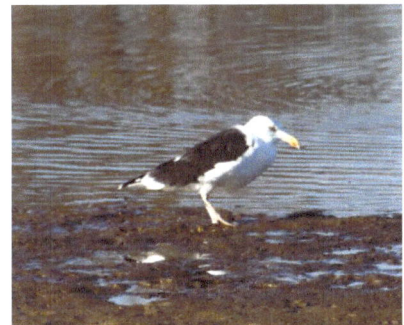 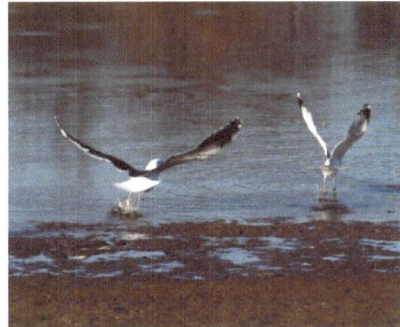

Greater Black-backed Gull

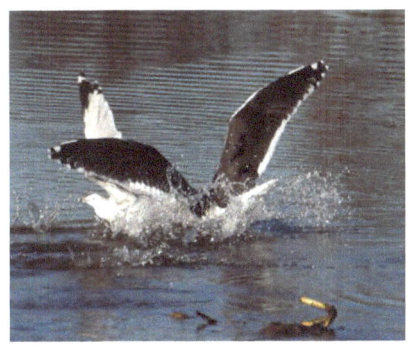 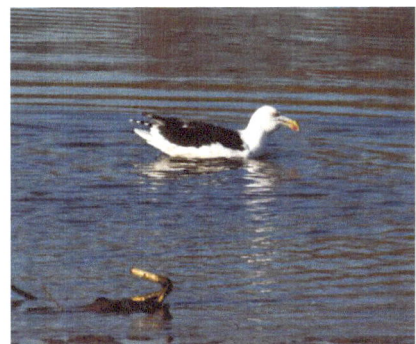

Chapter 8

The Usual Suspects

There are many birds that I see regularly on my walks. I call them the usual suspects. I tend to take them for granted because I think I can always get a good picture of them. The Red-winged Blackbird is one of them. They seem to always be around the ponds and lakes I frequent. This is a beautiful bird and one of the species where the female and the male are quite different. As I looked through my pictures I realized that I didn't have any pictures of the female.

Red-winged Blackbird (male)

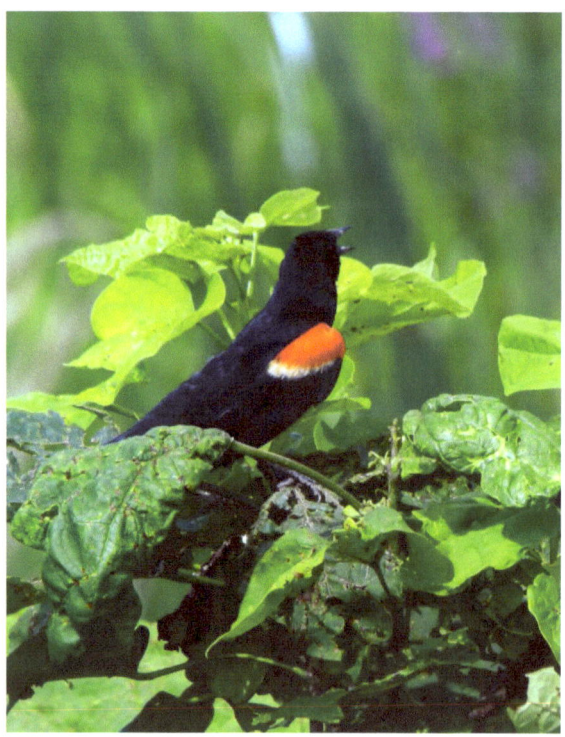

The Northern Cardinals are all over this area. This is one of the first birds I learned by its call. They call and respond a lot and fly to the calls of other cardinals. These are some of the most recognizable and beautiful of all the US birds.

(male)　　　Northern Cardinal　　(female)

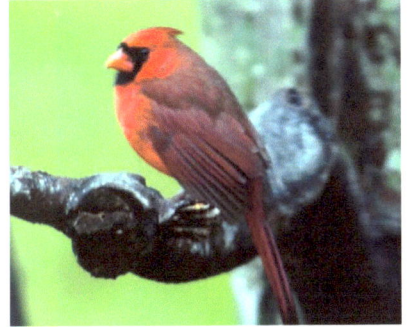
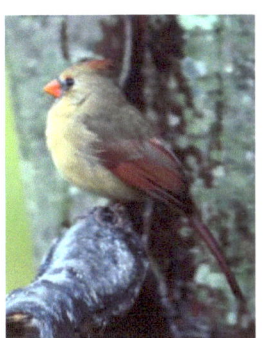

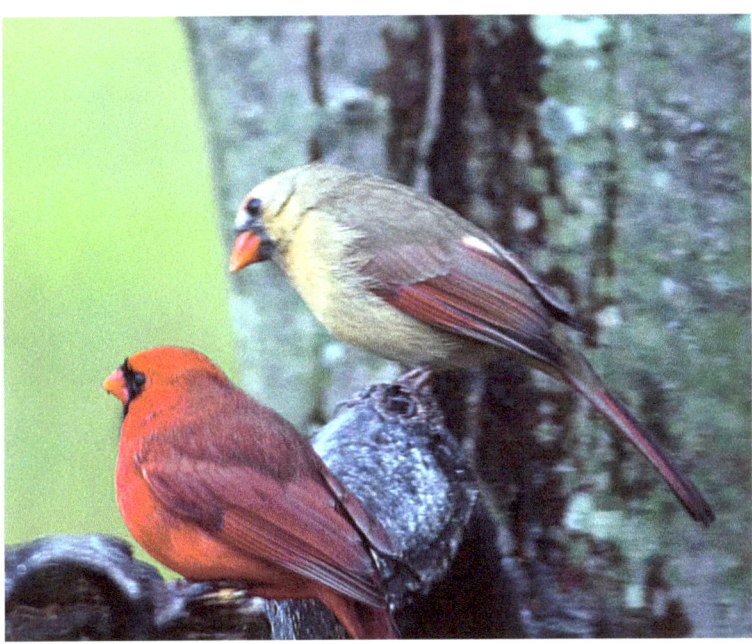

The European Starling is another bird that I run into frequently. They are very unusual in appearance. It is said thet they were native to Europe. They were introduced in the US and rapidly spread in geography and in numbers.

European Starlings

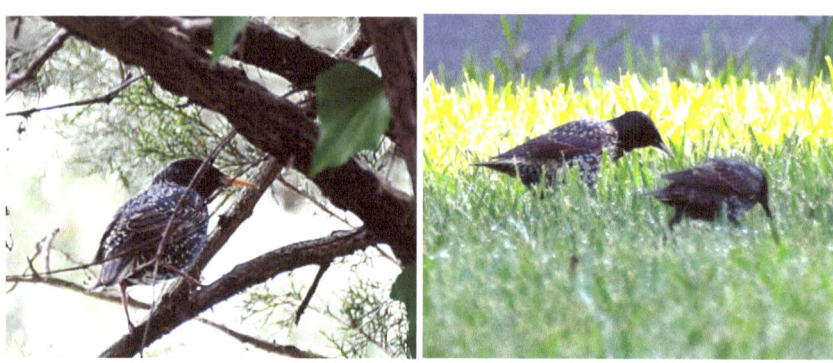

Mourning Doves are also plentiful in my neighborhood. They are usually found in pairs. I have taken a lot of pictures of them. Now I only take them when I can get an unusual shot.

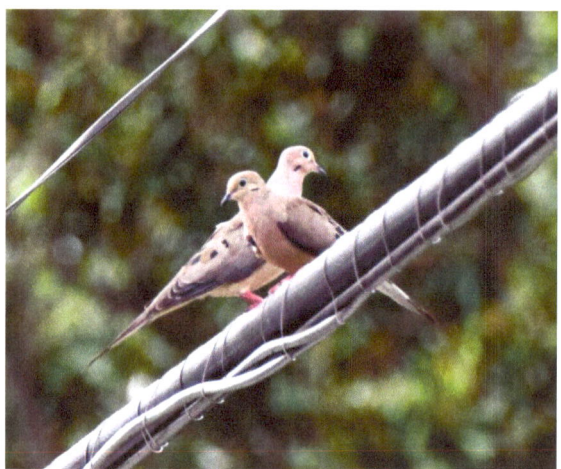

Rock Doves were just called pigeons when I was young. When I go into DC I see them a lot. My son had a field trip to the Capitol where I took this shot.

Rock Dove

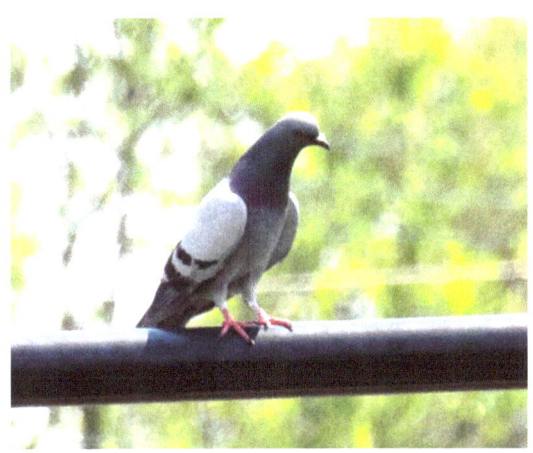

Some sparrows are native. There are so many species that I really take them for granted. They can be found in small groups or large flocks. These birds like to sing and will come and eat the seeds that drop from my bird feeders. Some sparrows migrate here and come and go.

Song Sparrow   Chipping Sparrow

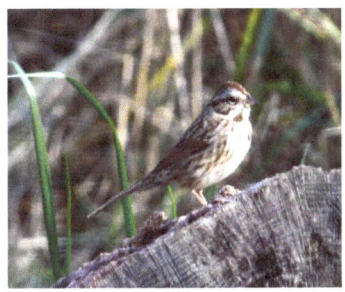   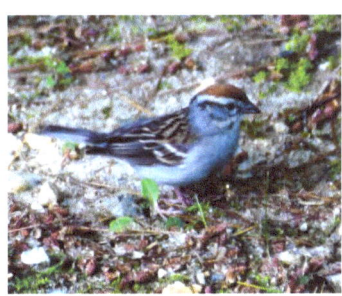

House Sparrow   White-throated Sparrow

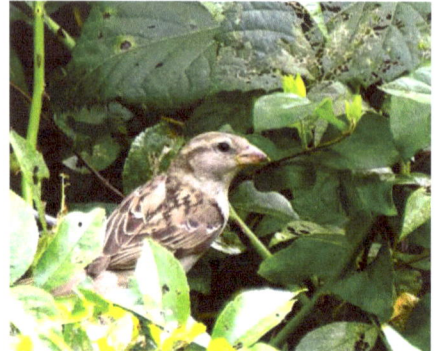 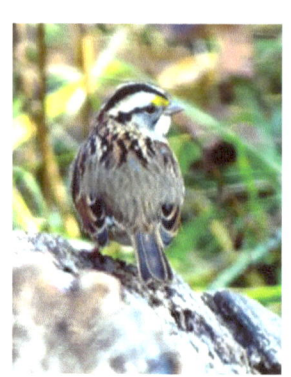

Canadian Geese are seen so frequently in my area, I doubt if they ever go back to Canada. It is a magnificent bird. They seem to be very adaptable. They are very common on the golf courses here where there is a lot of water.

Canada Goose

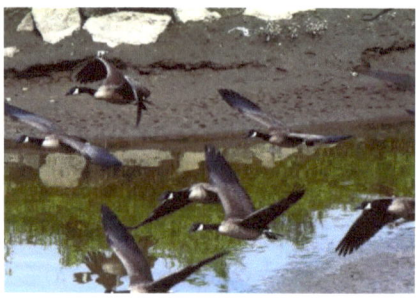 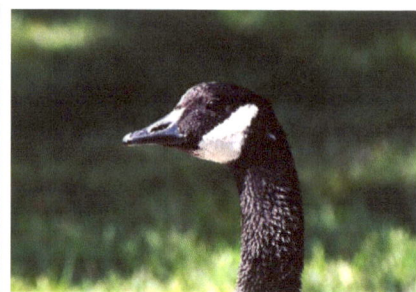

Chapter 9

New Areas

Most of the pictures I have shown were taken within three miles of my house. This is where I take most of my pictures and has been good enough for me to get over 70 different species of birds. Now I try to take my camera where ever I go. This chapter is about some of the birds I got in other areas.

My family went on vacation in Saffire Valley, NC. It is a beautiful place to go and get away from it all. It is in the mountains of North Carolina not far from Asheville, North Carolina.

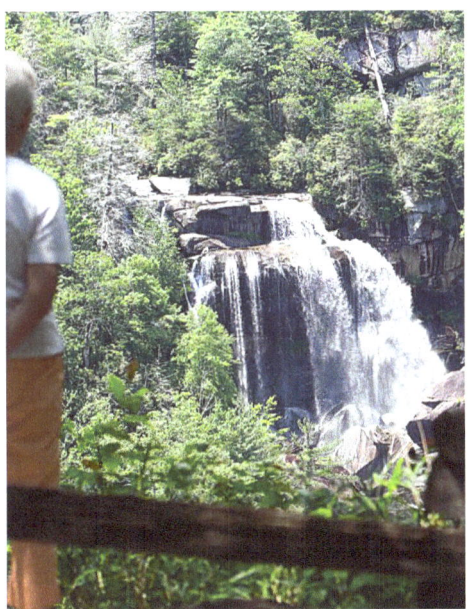

It was our only vacation where we were warned about bears. There was evidence of them by the paw marks all over the trash cans.

It also made for some interesting walks. The first bird I saw that interest me was the Eastern Bluebird. It was very colorful and I had never seen one before this trip.

Eastern Bluebird

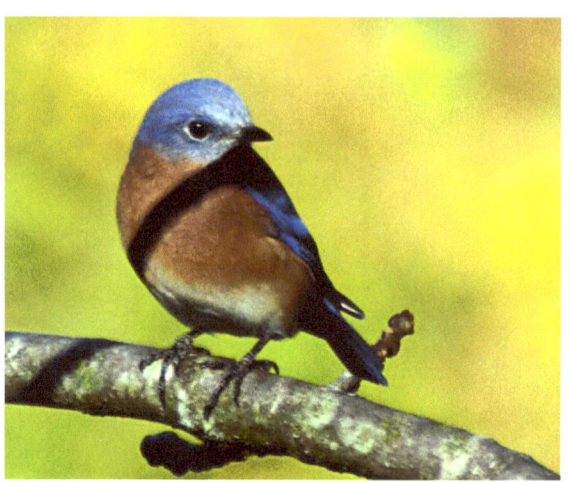

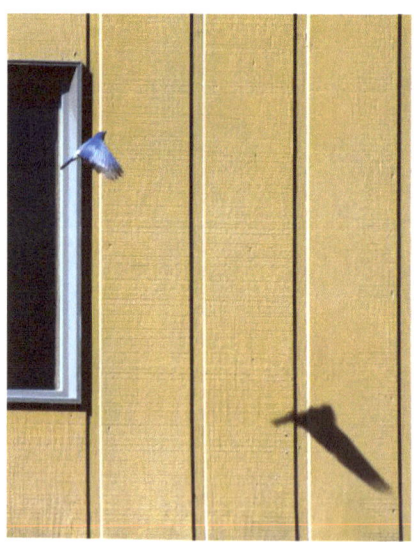

I saw many American Robins feeding in a field. They were all over the mountain in early summer. This is where I first became aware of bird behavior. I was catching the birding bug.

American Robin

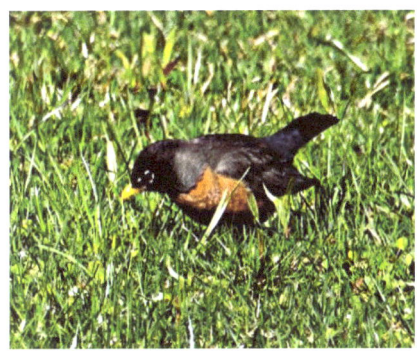 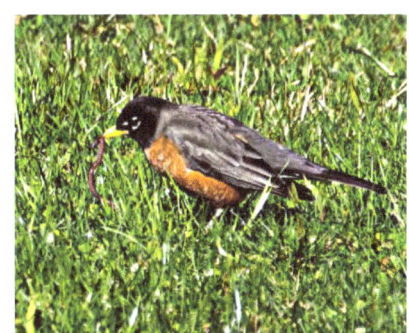

I saw my first White Breasted Nuthatch here. I also saw a huge Raven right outside my condo window. His nest must have been in this tree because he posed for me for a long time.

Common Raven

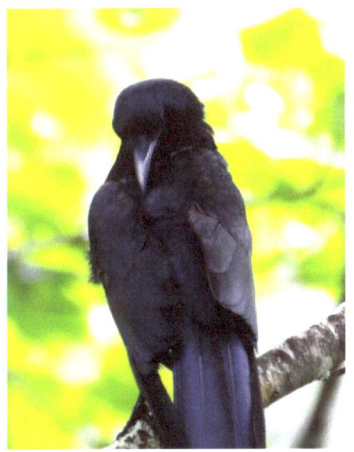 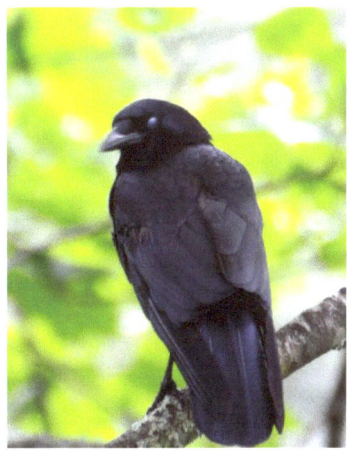

The Eastern Towhee is a bird that I rarely see in my area. It is usually on the ground or in thicket where it is hard to get a good photo. I got lucky with this shot.

Eastern Towhee

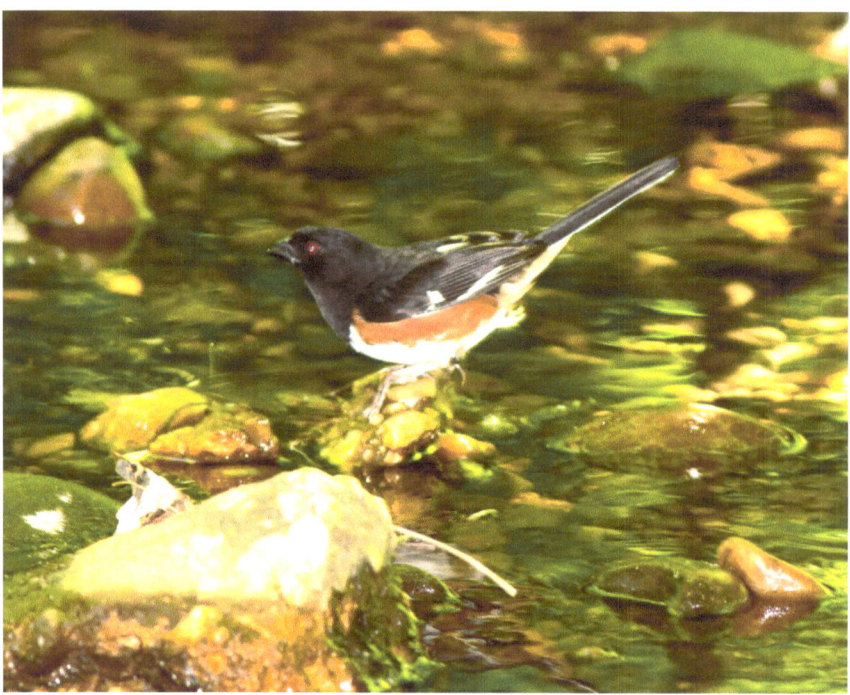

I had fun in the mountains and this is one of the reasons I started carrying my camera everywhere I went. I had a quick business trip to Florida one week. I didn't really think I would get a chance to take pictures. After work my colleague and I went to the beach to look for birds. It was a very slow day and then something magical happened. A flock of Pelicans flew by us. I was in general mode and just started shooting. I was happy to get a few good shots.

Brown Pelican

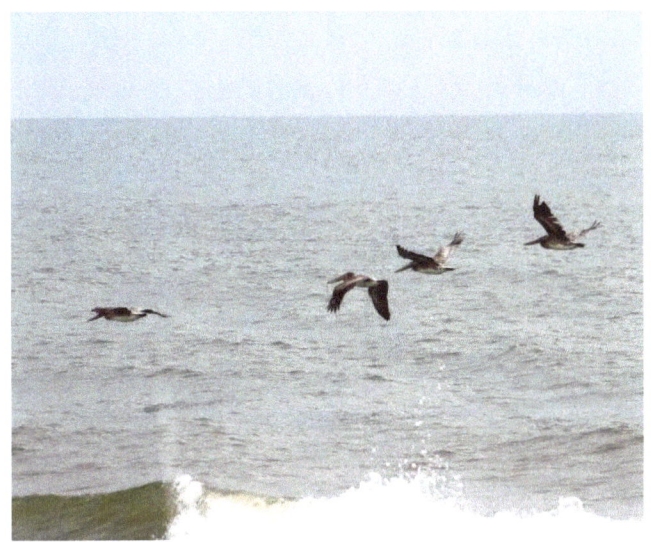

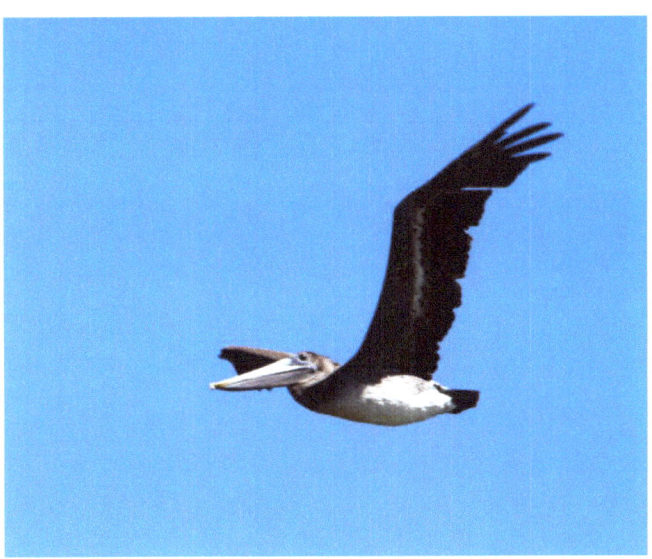

I also got a very small Blue Jay one morning before work. Believe it or not I was just as happy to get the Blue Jay as the Peligans. **TIP#27-It never ceases to amaze me how joyful small moments have been.** I had never seen a pelican before and was very happy to see them flying by me. I was equally happy to get the small Blue Jay. Taking pictures is a technical process and an art. I have skills in this area honed from my childhood experience starting with a Polaroid camera. I then went to a cheap 35mm film camera and finally to a professional Digital SLR Camera. I have always loved taking pictures and the reaction of others as they looked at the pictures. Birding is different. All of the above applies but there is a very spiritual aspect of birding for me. It is the interaction with nature and the surprises that happen regularly that I cherish.

Blue Jay

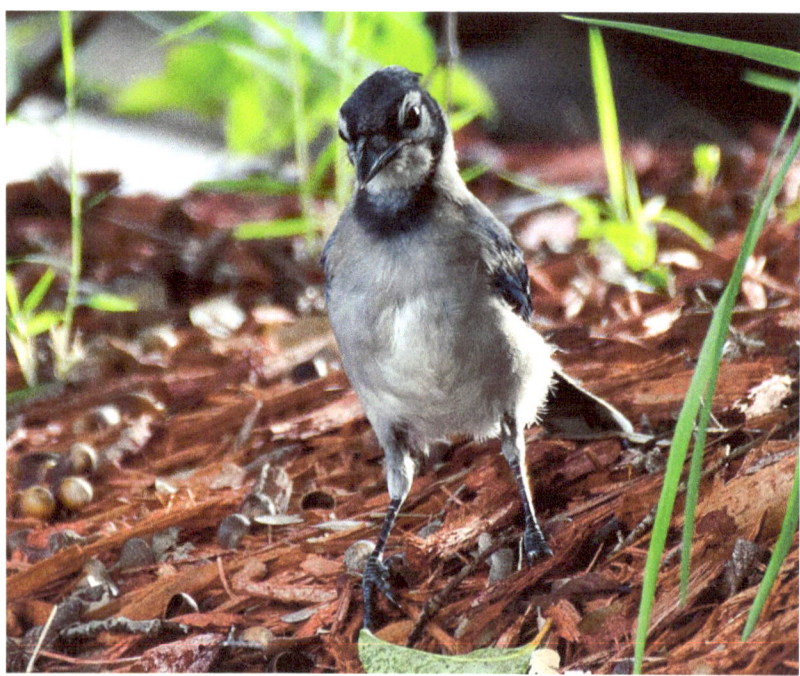

Chapter 10

What Else Is Out There

    I was glad to be home. I don't get much time when I'm on the road to take pictures. Work is the conundrum of modern society. It seems many of us are working harder and enjoying it less. The entire culture seems to revolve around our jobs and our self esteem is dependent on our position in a company. I was starting to feel I was getting to the end of my career without reaching some of my goals. The recession has exasperated this situation as many people have done "everything right " but find themselves out of work. Some have skill sets that have made them very desirable to employers in the past. Now they have been looking for work for years and have not been able to replace the income they once enjoyed.

    Birding has helped me deal with this better. Nature has a set of rules that are consistent and predictable. While I'm looking for birds I became aware of other things that were hidden from me before. One obvious one is that my house is on the flight map between Thurgood Marshal BWI and Reagan National Airports. I see a lot of planes everyday while on my walks. I also noticed that you can hear electricity flowing through the lines near the path I walk. I have never been an environmentalist but the more I am connected with nature the more I want to make sure I do my part to take care of it.

    I am also more aware of the landscapes around me. I will walk through neighborhoods near me that I wasn't interested in before looking for birds. One of the neighborhoods had a large lake that is more of a marsh now. There was once a huge lake there but not much opportunity for water fowl. One day I was talking to some cyclists that told me about a huge lake where there were many ducks and geese. I couldn't picture where they were describing. I was determined to find this area. On my next walk I followed their directions to the letter. I had walked all over this neighborhood in the past. Then I turned down a street that I had never walked before. After about 15 minutes I came upon a huge lake with ducks and geese as promised. **TIP#28 –Revisit areas periodically to see if the environment has become more Bird friendly.** Below are the pictues I got of the Hooded Merganser at this lake.

Hooded Merganser (male)   Hooded Merganser(female)

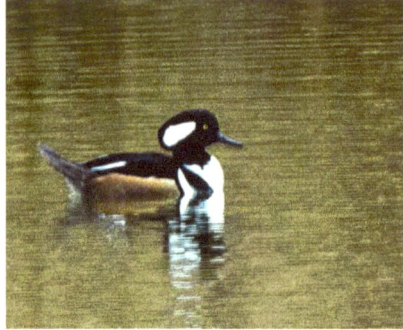 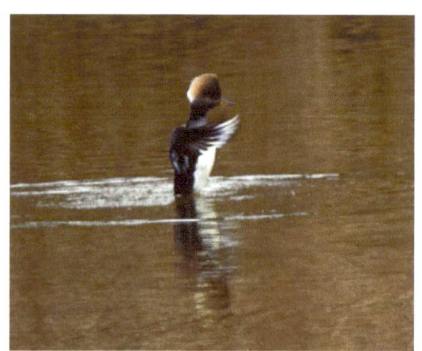

This is a beautiful duck. As usual the male is the more colorful of the species. He has an unusual habit that I learned by observing them. He will sometimes swim with his beak pointed down which makes the white mark on his head appear larger. I thought it was cool.

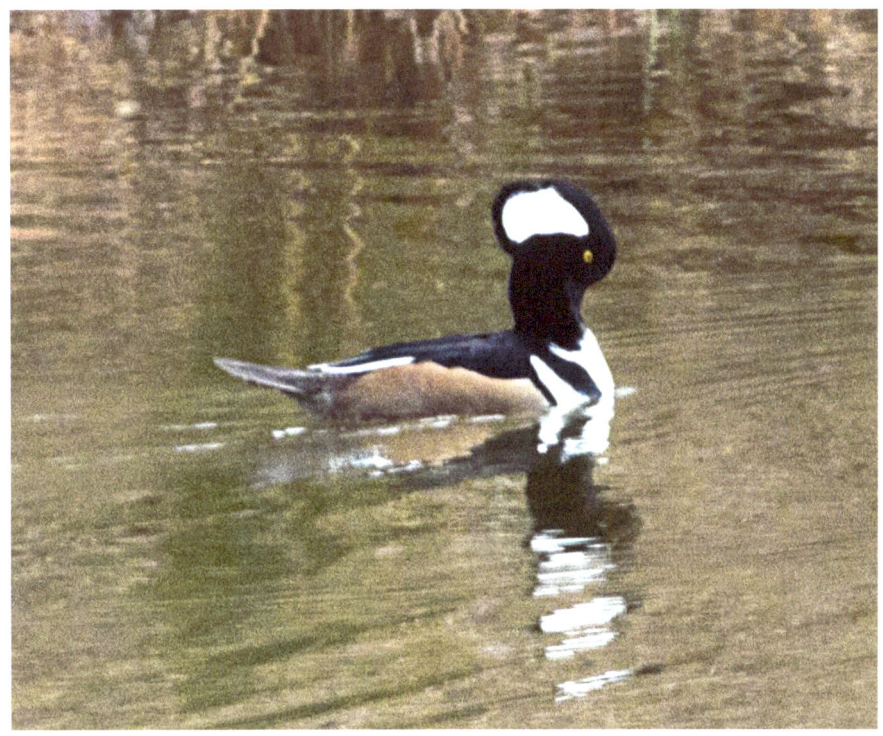

Discovering such a good habitat for birding made me rethink the entire area. I had to stop remembering it the way it was when I was a child and actually walk these areas. As a result I went off the path and walked further back into the neighborhood. I noticed that the lake I thought was dried up was further back in the neighborhood and was very vibrant. I began to walk this area and saw many birds regularly that I had seen only occasionally. Now I figured this is why I would see the Eagles in an area that didn't have water. Now I was on a mission to find the eagles' nest (aerie).

I began to walk the neighborhood and go down side streets to see which ones dead ended on the lake. One day while exploring I saw a Bald

Eagle high in a tree near the lake. I got a few pix but knew I needed a better lens to bring them in closer. I also knew that I would need a tripod. I had to make an investment and it would not be cheap. I decided to buy a 400mm prime lens. I have a nice 70-300mm lens but I thought I could improve the reach and the quality. Knowing that eagles mate early in the season I knew I needed to act quickly. **TIP#29 –Use all of your resources when buying equipment for Birding.** There are video reviews and blogs on the internet that discuss the pros and cons of this equipment.

I couldn't wait to use my new lens. It didn't take long before I got a good chance. I saw an American Bald eagle perched on a high branch. I got a lot of good shots. The light wasn't perfect but it was good. When the Eagle flew off I got some shots. Then the miracle. He flew onto the nest where the female was seated. I got two American Bald Eagles in an eagle's Aerie (nest). It's funny how things and events work together. Ask and it shall be given.

American Bald Eagle pair

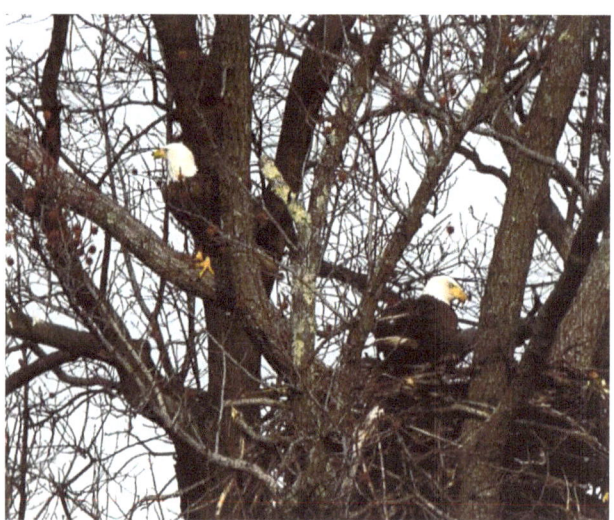

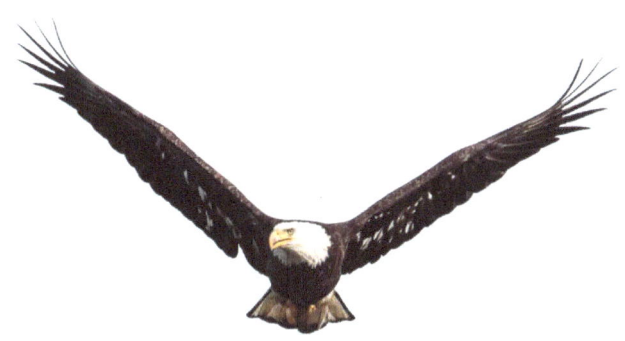

Now I have eagles on the brain. I can't wait for the sun to come out so I can go back and photograph the eagles. I'm wondering if they might have eggs in the nest. How could I earn the $15,000.00 needed to get a high quality 600mm lens? It was all very powerful how much this event meant to me. Just when I thought I had it down I went a week without a single American Bald Eagle sighting. So much for my expertise.

    I used this time to get back to a more normal sense of being. I walked some of my regular treks and saw old species in a new light. Having better equipment has made it much more enjoyable. It also improved my eye and made me less satisfied with some of my earlier pictures. Sharpness was a big factor. The Better lenses make sharper pictures. The other difference was color variation. I know my newer pictures require less correction in Photo editing software. **TIP#30-There is a reason why Professional Wildlife Photographers get paid for their pictures.** It is a hard job and you have to devote your life to it to get to that level. Make sure you keep in mind the amount of time and money you can devote to your HOBBY.

I finally saw the movie The Big Year. This was a great movie. I will not spoil it but it helps put birding in perspective for me. I appreciate the insight into the extreme end of the Hobby and how to keep a balance in my journey.

This experience made me want to find a Hawks nest. I have yet to find one but the hunt has netted some good photos. I got this Red-tailed Hawk while I was walking to a Doctor's office for a visit.

Red-tailed Hawk

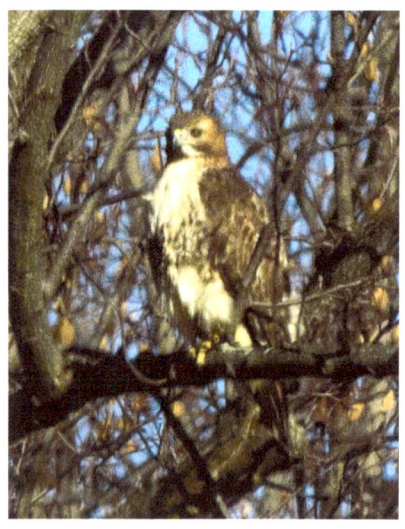
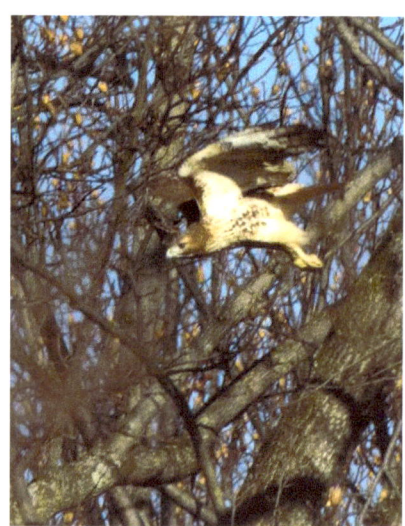

Red-tailed Hawk Pair

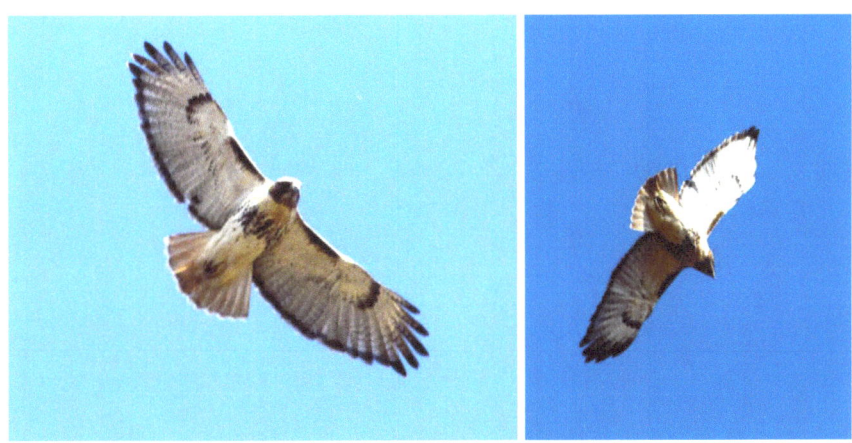

I think I have a lead on a Red-Shouldered Hawk's nest. I have seen the same hawk in a tree near a shopping center by my house. I will need to confirm it by seeing him go into the nest one evening

Red-shouldered Hawk

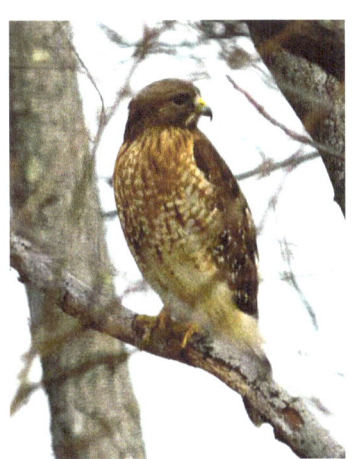

I also got a series of pictures of a Downey Woodpecker pecking out a hole deep inside a tree. I will keep an eye out for little ones here later in the season.

Downey Woodpecker

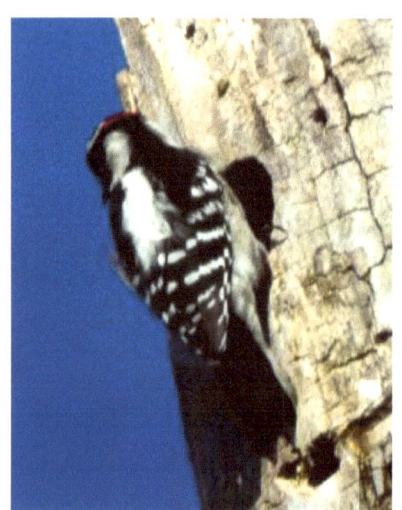
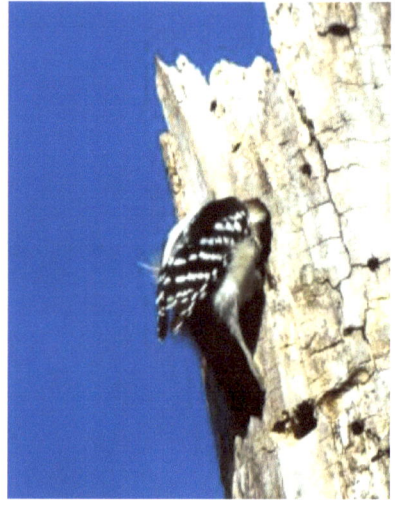
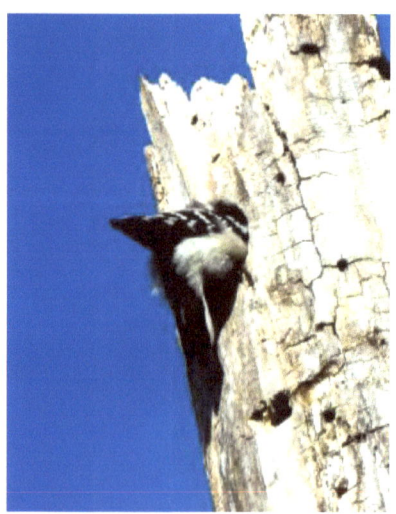

Chapter 11

They Quack Me Up

I wanted to talk a little specifically about waterfowl. This is a subject that caught me off guard because it is so different from my walks through the woods. I have gotten pictures at small ponds but now know that there are many different water habitats where I have gotten good shots of ducks and other waterfowl.

I heard a strange noise one day as I was walking past a small pond. I was on the way to a large lake where I had seen an Osprey nest. I looked but didn't find the source of the noise. After a while I saw the most beautiful duck. I had seen pictures of them but this was the first one I saw in the wild. The noise came from a male Wood Duck. I was fascinated by the unusual colors separated by white. I almost forgot about the Osprey. As I moved to get closer the Wood Duck flew away. This made me more determined to get a good picture. I asked a lot of birders if they had gotten Wood Duck pictures. Some said they were very wary of people. Others said they were tame in areas where they were exposed to a lot of people. **TIP#31-Somes birds act very differently in different environments.** I went to all the places where people told me they saw Wood Ducks but could never get close. I finally wised up and went to the place where I was told the Wood Ducks would pose. To my surprise I saw a male and female Wood Duck together. I was surprised that they didn't fly away like I expected. I got close and got these pictures.

| Male | Wood Duck | Female |

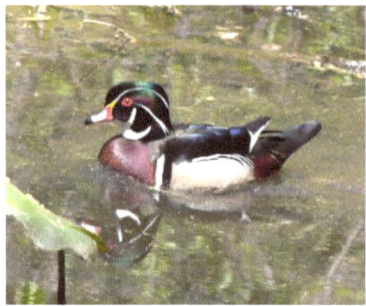 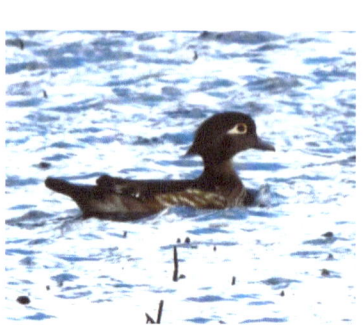

      This put me on a mission to find as many ducks as possible. I went back to my bass fishing days and began to frequent Lake Artemesia. This one spot became my go to place for new duck species. In one month I saw Ring-neck Ducks, American Coot, and Greater and Lesser Scaups. There were Mallards there also. It seemed that everytime I went there I would see something new.

Ring-necked Duck   American Coot

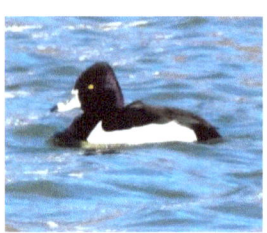 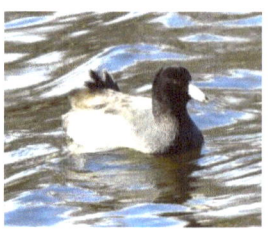

Greater Scaup   Lesser Scaup

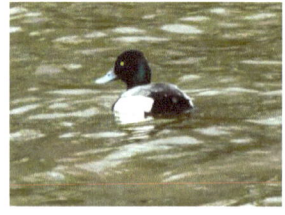 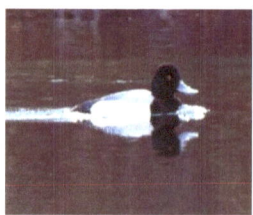

I wanted to get as many ducks as possible while I was on a roll. One day I saw a Redhead Duck. This is a duck that isn't as common in my area. It took me several hours to get a good shot.

Redhead Duck

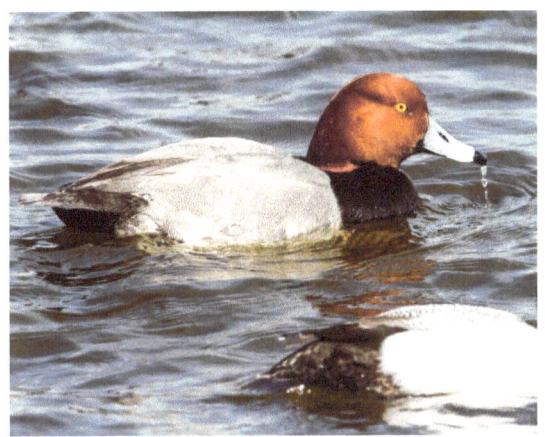

Common Shoveler

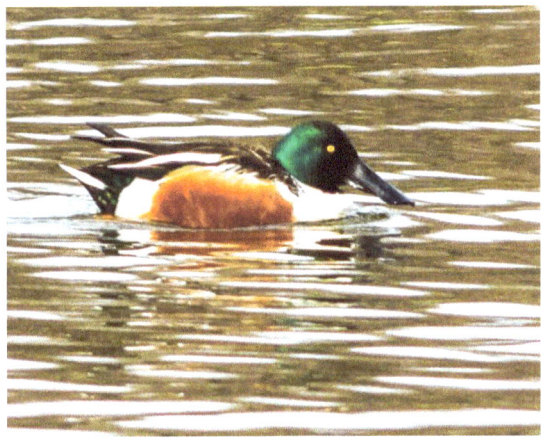

Sometimes a day of birding just doesn't go as planned. I went to a place where I usually saw a lot of ducks and got nothing. A few Mallards and Ring-necked Ducks but nothing unusual. I heard a Belted Kingfisher and finally spotted where he was. I knew I could get a good picture if I walked about a quarter of a mile around the Lake. When I got there he didn't fly off as usual. I noticed he was looking at something but thought it was a crawfish or something. When I looked down I saw a Canvasback Duck. This was my first one so I was excited about it. I got a few shots then moved in closer. I was very happy with the pix I got. This was an unexpected treat. **TIP#32-Some times you get something exotic when you least expect it.**

    I was well on my way to a good portfolio of ducks so I felt I could relax and go back to my discovery walks.

Canvasback Duck

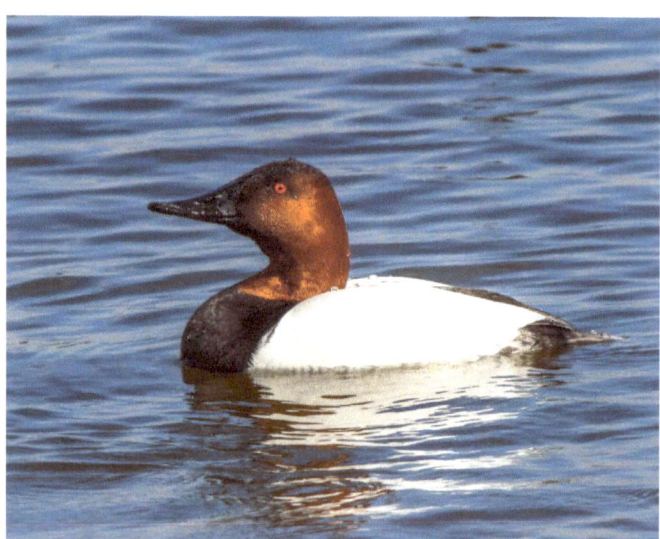

Chapter 12

Friends and Strangers

I wanted to say a word about the many people I have met on the paths and walkways. We are living in a constant news cycle. We are reminded every day about the dangers of modern life. It is always amazing to me the horrendous acts human beings do to other human beings. I have just witnessed the re-election of the first African American President of the United States. My joy was soon tempered with the opposition the President faced when the Ceremony was over. I was glad to turn the TV off and go on my walks.

The wintertime is a great time to reflect. The trees have lost their leaves and the traffic on the paths has slowed to a crawl. Now the real warriors are out doing their thing. I am always amazed by the good hearted people I meet. I speak to everyone and my 400mm lens is a great conversation starter. These strangers are always willing to tell me where they saw an unusual bird. They are very warm and sometimes the conversation turns to life and life lessons. It is during these times that I get back in touch with the idea that there are good people in the world. I spoke to a woman in her 70's visiting her sick sister and taking advantage of the path. Without her saying a word about it I was struck with how important our health is and what a blessing it is that we have loved ones that care about us.

I met a couple that had been married for a lot of years and still found time to go for walks together. They were interested in my pictures and told me the part of the path where they frequently saw Cardinals. They said they try to take a walk together everyday.

One cyclist I see almost everyday. He always stops to greet me and to see what I am shooting on that particular day.

Some days I run into people from my past that I haven't seen in years. I ran into my best friend's brother Darryl that got me into cycling. We talked about the 50 mile rides we used to take. We laughed about how he rode us into the ground and taught us that you have to keep enough in the tank for the ride back home.

I regularly see a friend John from high school. He was a very good athlete and was always in good shape. I like to see him because he fills me in on some of our old friends and usually has good info on where birds are hanging out. He also looks like he did when we were in school. He has taken his health seriously and is an inspiration. We all talk about health but he lives it and takes time out to make sure he stays in shape and communes with nature.

The birders are the best of all. They are so helpful and have provided me with so much information. It is always shared freely and lovingly. Now I can watch the news and know that there are still people out there that care about others. People that will help without asking for anything in return. One birder told me about the Audubon Society meetings and then proceded to show me where the Eagles nest was in our area. I returned the favor by taking her into the neighborhood and showing her how to get to the back side of a lake.

The birds have helped me get more in touch with nature and people. I'm beginning to think that they are the same thing and somehow

I forgot that connection. At least my walks give me less TV time and that is a good thing.

Just like the people, I have a new relationship with old birds. My goal this year is to get good pictures and great pictures. I want to do the birds justice by capturing their detail. The Carolina Wren is a bird that posed for me long enough to change my camera settings and get into better position to take advantage of the light. I finally think I got a great picture.

Carolina Wren

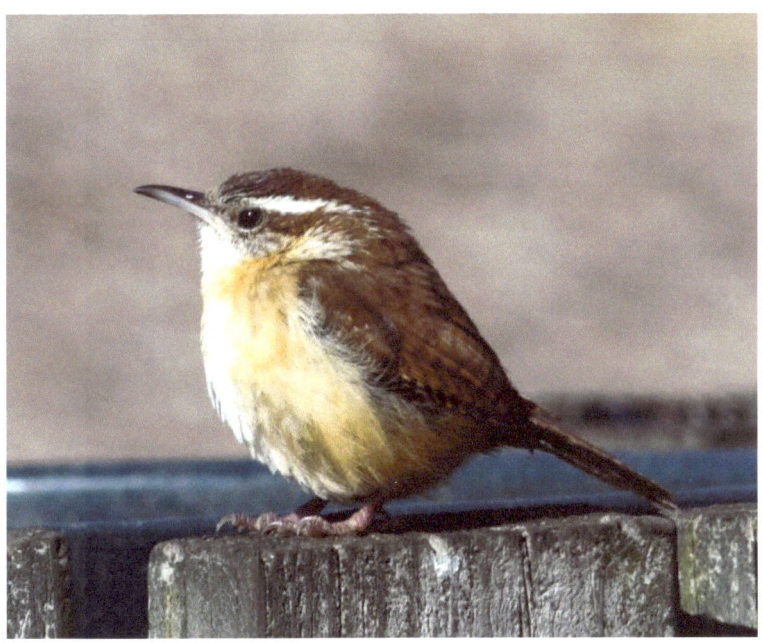

I have increased my level of exercise. Not only does my lens weigh more but I always carry a tripop/Gimbal head with me wherever I go. Here is a picture I got with ice on the pond.

Immature Ring-billed Gull

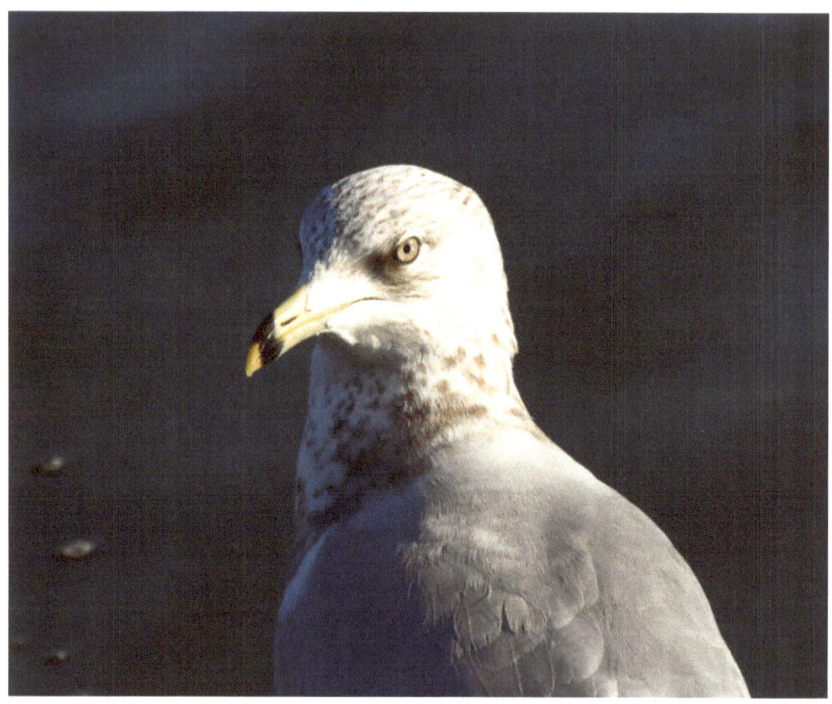

Mallard Ducks are plentiful here. Check out this picture of a colorful pair.

Mallard Ducks

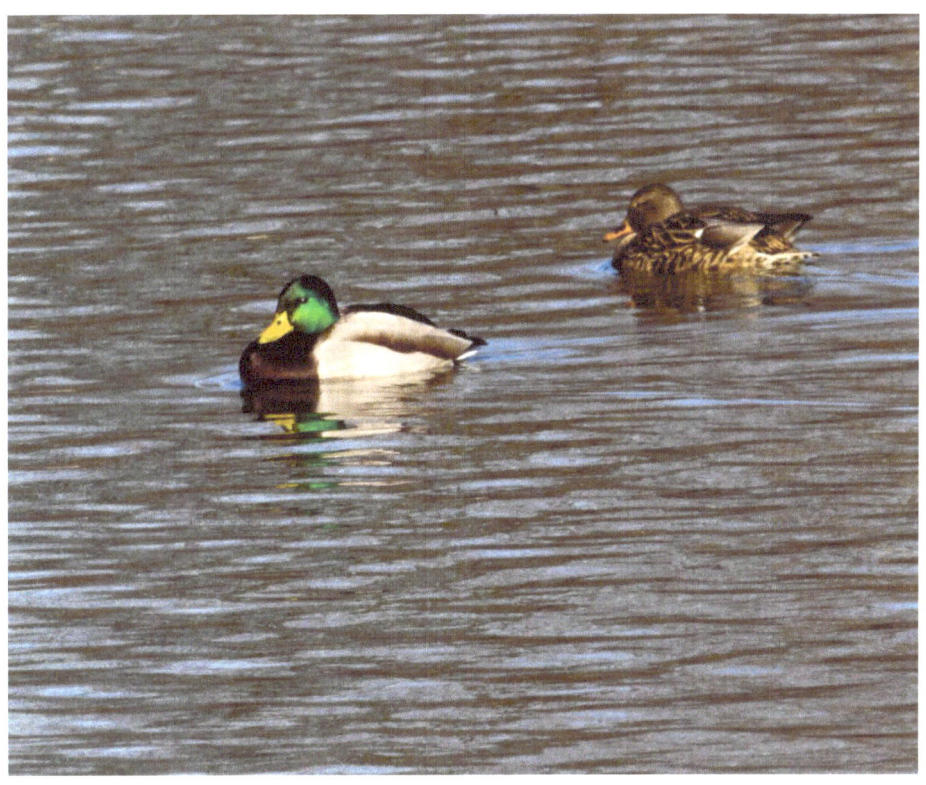

Chapter 13

Warblers

I have saved this chapter for late in the book. With the exception of a lot of the duck species, most of the birds in this book are around most of the year. Warblers are an exception. Most of these birds are only around during their migration. I would see them occasionally but had a very small sampling of warblers in my photos. I made a conscious effort to change this. I knew I needed help and turned to the local Audubon Society. They have bird walks and counts. They are a major resource and can help you spot and expand your knowledge of different species.

I made sure my dues were up to date and started going on these walks to get as many Warblers as I could. **TIP#33-Spend time with local experts to improve your Birding Skills.** Once I got the first colorful Warbler to pose for me I was hooked.

Prothonotary Warbler

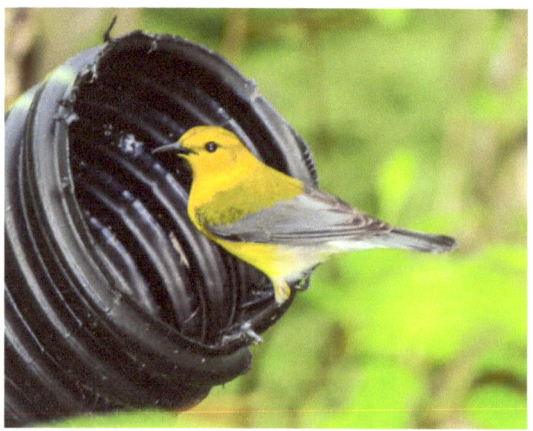

These birds are loved by many for their beauty and elusiveness. Each one made the surprise of the next all the more fun. I started going to Rock Creek Park in Washington DC. This is a stopover for many migrating Warblers. I got this shot thanks to a very observant Birder out for a morning walk with his wife.

Magnolia Warbler

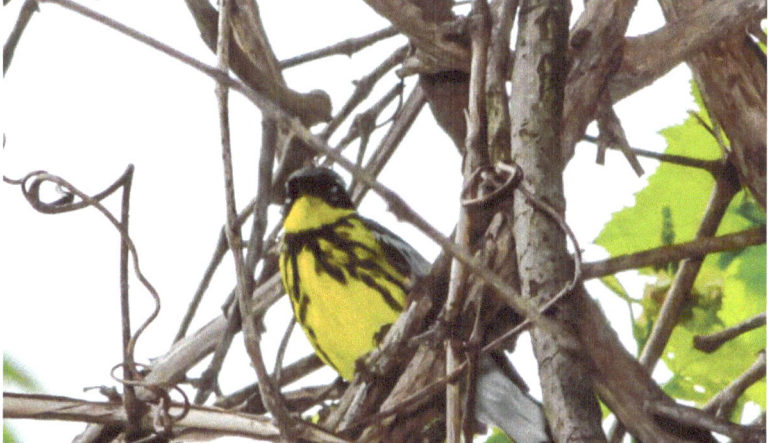

I was given a tip about a stream that was known for bathing Warblers. It was about ½ hr. drive so I gave it a shot. This beatiful bird was taken there.

Black-throated Blue Warbler

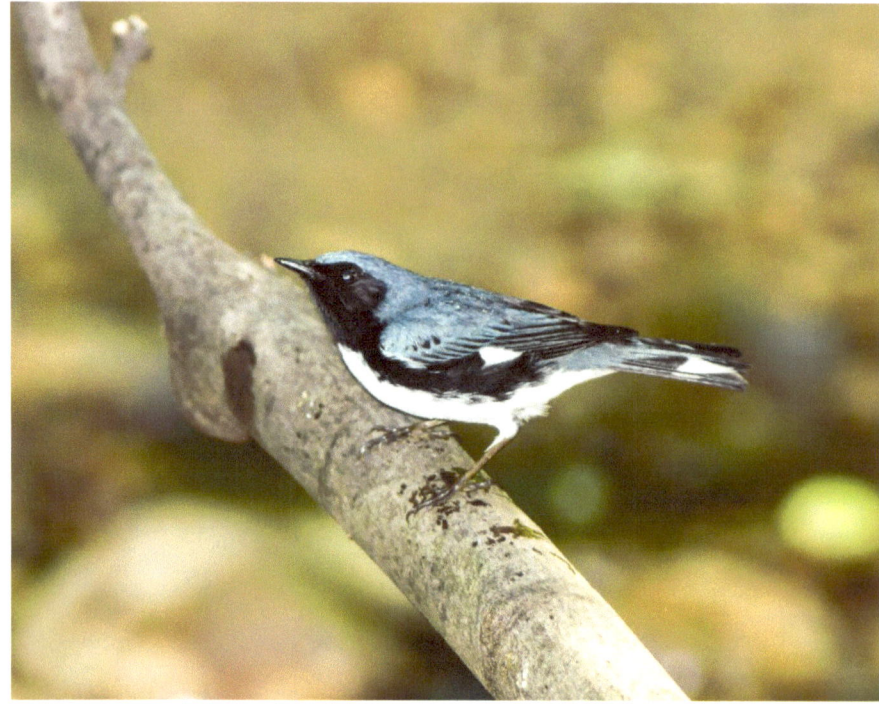

    This is a very popular spot and I have met a lot of nice people there. I will make sure this is a regular stop when Warbler season arrives each year.

    Even the more common Warblers are pretty. This Common Yellowthroat came to the creek for a bath. Warblers are usually either high in the tree canopy or in the thick brush. This is a good spot to see them up close. They are also small birds so the closer you can get the better.

Common Yellowthroat (male)

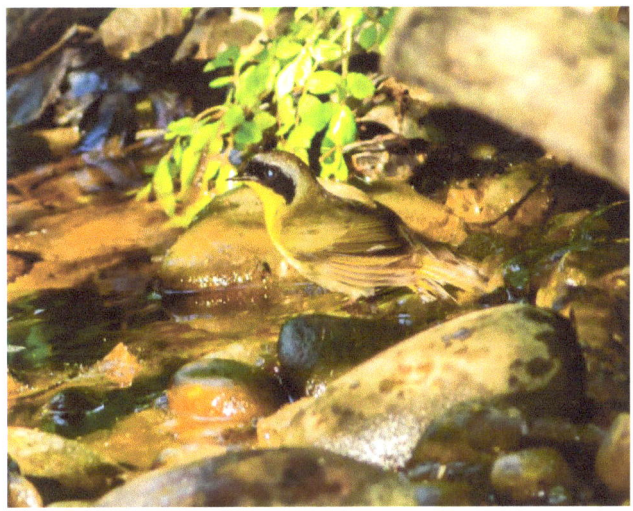

I was surprised to learn that a lot of birds that don't have warbler in their name are warblers too. The Northen Parula below is a good example.

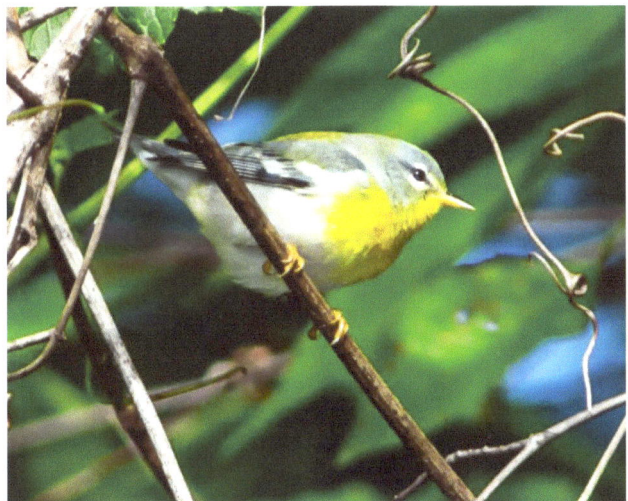

Chapter 14

Equipment

Equipment is very personal and will evoke passion especially in photographers. Since it is a beginners book I didn't want to make recommendations. I will say there are a lot of good brands out there and you should do your research before you buy. I will give some guidance.

Binoculars are probably the best way to start. It is easier to spot birds with a wider field of view. 8x42 is a good place to start. If you go for higher magnification you will also get more shake. This will make spotting birds more difficult.

You will also need to determine the gear ratio for the focus or get fixed focus Binoculars. This is again a personal preference but a medium gear ratio is a good place to start.

As I stated earlier, I use my eyes and a camera to spot birds. I started with a digital SLR camera and a 70-300mm f5.6 lens. It was a good place to start but I quickly wanted better equipment. My goal was to get large print quality photos.

If you want to share online and with friends on smartphones there are high quality digital compact cameras available. The Canon SX50 HS has a optical zoom range of 24-1200. I see a lot of Birders with this camera and they are very happy with the results, especially considering the price. It can get you close to the action and give you a record of what you saw without breaking the bank.

Professionals usally go for larger lenses and faster glass. The smallest f stop available is what makes a lens fast. f/2.8 is considered faster than f/5.6. 400mm focal length is a good Birder lens and comes in f/stops from f2.8-f5.6. This is the start of the Pro lenses and are very expensive. Zoom lenses offer greater flexibility but are usually not as fast or as sharp. They are also less expensive than Prime or fixed focal length lens.

Equipment is important but knowing how to use it is more important in my opinion. I have seen people with $8,000.00 worth of equipment that got poor results because they didn't understand how to use it. Get a good starter camera and lens and learn how to use the features. Learn how to get the best lighting and focus. Then learn which aperature and shutter speeds give you the results you want in different situations. Get a basic photo editing software and play with it to enhance your pictures. After you get the best photos with the gear you have, then you can move up in quality.

You can get good buys on used equipment but make sure you buy from a trusted source. Talk to other birders. As there skills increase they will often sell their old gear to upgrade to better equipment. It might not be new but it will be new to you.

Chapter 15

Final Chapter

I think this is a good place to end. Although it is only the beginning of my Birding Journey it is the end of this book. I wanted to share my experiences and knowledge of birding and photography. I hope it has been a help. There were a lot of things I learned that weren't in any of the books I was reading. My passion for birding and the joy I felt learning it made me want to share.

This book also has to do with the second chance I was given. I am now a 6 year Cancer Survivor. It gave me a better sense of my own mortality and that I was missing out on many of the real pleasures of life. I am more aware of the feelings of my family and friends. I am more aware of the contribution I make in the workplace. And I am more aware of the miracles around me and the vastness and wonder of the world I live in. I hope you enjoyed this book as much as I enjoyed the journey that inspired me to write it.

If you would like to see more of my pictures please visit me at:
www.threeceemedia.net.

TIPS

TIP#1-Keep it fun

TIP#2-You can learn a lot by just doing it

TIP#3-Birding doesn't lend itself well to perfection

TIP #4-The lighting is best when you shoot down your shadow line

TIP#5-Make sure you get a good shot before you start making changes to your camera settings

TIP#6-Always back up your photos

TIP#7-Be aware of your surroundings

TIP #8-Sometimes you have to relax your focus and let the Birds come to you

TIP#9-Don't beat yourself up if you miss a good picture

TIP#10-Make your own decisions about your Birding Journey

TIP#11-All birds can help you in your Birding Journey

TIP#12-When you take group bird pictures, make sure you check every individual bird

TIP#13-Many different species of birds frequent the same habitat

TIP#14 –Use a tripod if you can to get the best pictures

TIP#15-There is a lot of information out there about birds.

TIPS

TIP#16-Sometimes you have to put a lot of variables together to identify a bird at a distance

TIP#17-Learn to anticipate where the bird will land for better photos

TIP#18-Sometimes you have to let the action come to you

TIP#19-Little Miracles happen every day

TIP#20-Keep a folder of Birds you can't identify for further study

TIP#21-Birding is an activity that you can involve your entire family

TIP#22-Set up your camera for two different shooting conditions. Full screen Focus and Single point Focus

. TIP#23-Enjoy the moment

TIP# 24- Follow the Boy Scout Pledge and always be prepared. You never know when you will get the chance of a lifetime

TIP#25-Its not cheating to get great pictures at a birdfeeder

. TIP#26-Learning a birds behavior will help you to get more interesting pictures

TIP#27-It never ceases to amaze me how joyful small moments have been

TIP#28 –Revisit areas periodically to see if the environment has become more Bird friendly

TIP#29 –Use all of your resources when buying equipment for Birding

TIPS

TIP#30-There is a reason why Professional Wildlife Photographers get paid for their pictures

TIP#31-Somes birds act very differently in different

TIP#32-Some times you get something exotic when you least expect it

TIP#33-Spend time with local experts to improve your Birding Skills

INDEX

American Bald Eagle, 6, 15, 34, 61, 62

Northern Cardinal, 38, 48

American Coot, 67

American Crow, 45

American Goldfinch, 37, 38

American Robin, 54

Belted Kingfisher, 17, 18

Black Vulture, 14

Blue Jay, 23, 24, 25, 57

Brown Pelican, 56

Brown Thrasher, 11

Canada Goose, 51

Common Raven, 54

Ducks

    Canvasback. 69

    Common Shoveler, 68

    Hooded Merganzer, 59, 60

    Mallard Duck, 21, 74

INDEX cont.

Redhead, 68

Ring-necked Duck, 67

Scaups,

    Lesser Scaup. 67

    Greater Scaup, 67

    Wood Duck, 67

Eastern Bluebird, 53

Eastern Towhee, 55

European Starling, 11, 49

Finch

    House Finch, 38

    Purple Finch, 38

Gray Catbird, 44

Gulls

    Greater Black-backed Gull, 46

Hawks

    Red-shouldered Hawk, 13, 33, 64

    Red-tailed Hawk, 33, 63, 64

INDEX cont.

Northern Cardinal, 38, 48

Northern Mockingbird, 43

Osprey, 35, 36

Red-throated Hummingbird, 26

Red-winged Blackbird, 47

Sparrows

    Chipping Sparrow, 50

    House Sparrow, 51

    Song Sparrow, 50

    White-throated Sparrow, 51

TIPS, 82, 83, 84

Tufted Titmouse, 40

White-breasted Nuthatch, 39

Warblers

    Black-throated Blue Warbler, 77

    Common Yellowthroat, 78

    Magnolia Warbler, 76

    Northern Parula, 78

Prothonotary Warbler, 75

INDEX cont.

Woodpeckers

    Downey Woodpecker, 27, 28, 31, 65

    Hairy Woodpecker, 31

    Northern Flicker, 8, 29

    Pileated Woodpecker, 9

    Red-Bellied Woodpecker, 31

    Yellow-bellied Sapsucker, 30

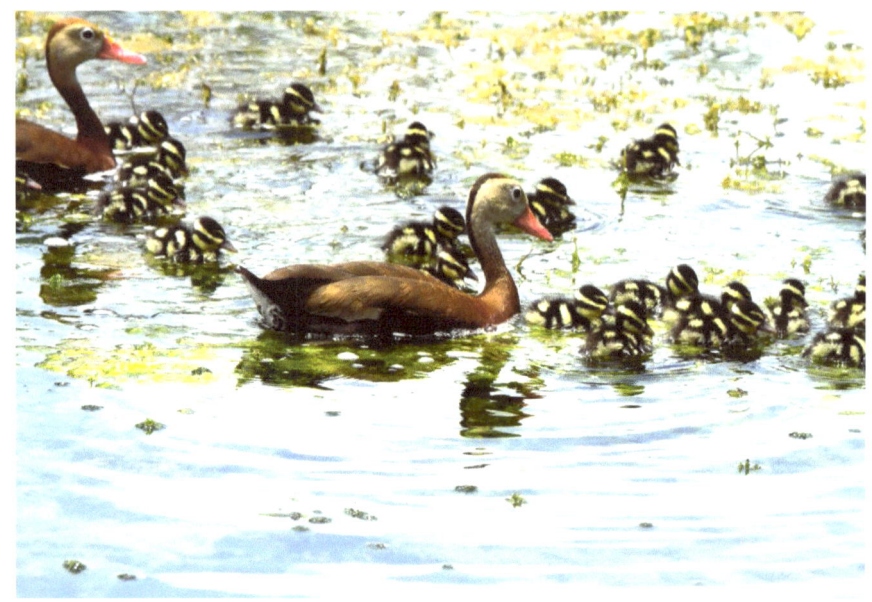

Birding for Beginners

A helpful guide for people entering the wonderful world of birding. This book is full of photographs and tips that will help you see more birds and photograph what you have seen. A must have how to book for Beginners that relates actual experiences without getting too technical.

www.ingramcontent.com/pod-product-compliance
Lightning Source LLC
Chambersburg PA
CBHW040222220526
45473CB00001B/88